Don Cassell is Chairman of the Law Board for the National Council for the Training of Journalists, with special responsibility for the photographic law syllabus and examination. He has specialised in the subject of photographic law for over 20 years.

Aside from his responsibilities with the NCTJ, over the years he has regularly featured as a legal advice columnist in such magazines as *Practical Photography* and *Photo Answers*.

The
Photographer
& the Law

Don Cassell

BFP BOOKS London

A catalogue record for this book is available from the British Library

ISBN 0-907297-44-7

First Published 1984
Second Edition 1989
Third Edition 1997

Published by BFP Books, Focus House, 497 Green Lanes, London N13 4BP. Design, typesetting and page layout by BFP Books. Main text set in New Century Schoolbook. Printed in Great Britain by Biddles Ltd, Guildford.

Acknowledgements

In writing the third edition of *The Photographer & the Law* I have received help from a number of sources including Charles Swan of the Simkins Partnership, solicitors specialising in copyright law, The Press Complaints Commission, The Photo Marketing Association International (UK) Ltd, the Patents Office, the Home Office and the Office of Fair Trading.

I am also greatly indebted to Walter Greenwood, author of *McNae's Essential Law for Journalists* which is about to have its 14th edition published, and to Stewart Gibson of BFP Books, my publisher.

However, the law is as I understand and believe it to be as of 30th April 1997 and any mistakes and/or errors are entirely mine.

Don Cassell

Contents

Preface

This book is written for all photographers, but especially for those working or intending to work in the media. In writing it I have tried to bring together the many strands of the law which may affect any photographer, whether he or she be a professional – working in or out of the media – or an enthusiastic amateur.

Copyright is a vital issue for all who seek to see their work published. Photographers' fundamental rights to profit from their work are now facing encroachments driven by new and rapidly changing technologies, so it is more essential than ever that photographers are aware of rights and remedies in this all-important area.

It may come as a surprise to many readers to realise how often in following their profession or hobby as photographers they can fall foul of various aspects of the law, either criminal or civil. Of course, all of us face this risk, quite often inadvertently, in our everyday life. But it is no exaggeration to say that, in certain circumstances, photographers may be at even greater risk.

Photographers – especially those working in the news media – are also frequently at risk of being manhandled and having expensive equipment damaged. How many are aware of their legal rights in these circumstances? This book points out these rights and discusses the remedies available.

Many photographers lack knowledge of consumer law as it affects their hobby or profession. Consequently, part of the book is devoted to outlining the rights which all of us have under what is popularly known as consumer law.

Legal rights are, however, accompanied by responsibilities towards others, and it is just as important that a photographer should be aware of the duty of care owed to those they may come across in following their hobby or profession.

Nevertheless, it must be stressed that this is not a "do it yourself" law book. It is said that "a lawyer who represents himself has a fool for a client", so the aim of this book is simply to explain the law in readily understandable language. Neither is the book a substitute for legal advice should it be necessary, but it is hoped that it will serve a useful dual purpose: firstly, to help photographers steer clear of legal pitfalls, and secondly, to inform them of their rights.

The public at large, including photographers, are often uncertain over the dividing line between criminal and civil law. The majority of situations that may affect photographers and discussed in this book come under civil rather than criminal law, and are known in legal parlance as "torts" – civil wrongs or injuries which give rise to remedies under civil law. Offences or injuries which may come under the criminal law are stated as such in the relevant text.

Differences in Scottish law are mentioned where relevant. However, much of the legislation covered in this book is United Kingdom law, common throughout the UK, while of course an increasing amount of legislation nowadays derives from the European Union.

There are references in this book to various offences which carry fines. As it has become the practice of Parliament that fines for certain offences be increased from time to time to keep pace with inflation, offences carrying financial penalties have been grouped together in bands or categories. This is so that one or all of the categories can be increased as and when it is thought necessary by Parliament, without having to introduce enabling legislation for each offence. For this reason, possible maximum fines are not mentioned in this book.

Finally, with a bow towards the current fad for political correctness, let me say that women make excellent photographers, especially in the media. Nevertheless, to save repetitious and boring use of the phrases "he/she", "his/hers", I plead the *Interpretation Act 1911* which states, *inter alia*, that the masculine shall include the feminine unless otherwise indicated.

1 The Meaning and Scope of Copyright

To understand the concept of copyright it is useful to trace its historical background, for so often in the mists of times long past are the first principle's of today's laws to be found.

In medieval days education was confined to a privileged few, many of whom were clerics. As education, such as it then was, spread, ever more people were able to read and write and even translate books from their original language – quite often, Latin – into English.

Those who had the ability to write and publish books banded together to form the Stationers Company – one of the oldest of Livery Companies – and the first concept of copyright appeared in 1533 when the company was granted protection against the importation of foreign books. In 1556 Queen Mary granted the Stationers Company the right to seek out and destroy books printed in contravention of the earlier statute.

Even today, under the *Copyright Designs and Patents Act 1988*, the owner of copyright has the right to apply to a court to seize copies which infringe copyright.

Mary, of course, had ulterior motives in granting the charter to the Stationers Company. She was, perhaps, more concerned to control any religious opposition to her reign, and by strengthening what was virtually a monopoly held by the Stationers Company, she was creating what was to become copyright: looked at from a simplistic point of view, all copyright is a legally backed monopoly to protect a person's intellectual property.

Mary was creating in effect a licence to publish, and for a book to be lawfully published it had to be entered in the register of the Stationers company. In the turbulent years that followed Mary, it paid Elizabeth and the subsequent Stuart kings to uphold such a licensing system as an effective way of controlling opposition in the form of the written word.

However, as the strength and power of Parliament increased at the expense of the monarchy it was inevitable that this situation could not continue. In 1664 Parliament refused to renew the licence the Stationers Company had held for 160 years.

To protect the intellectual property of writers, the first *Copyright Act* was passed in 1709, followed by another in 1814. In 1842 another Act repealed all previous Copyright Acts and became the governing statute for literary copyright until the Act of 1911.

Meanwhile, engravings, sculpture and musical and dramatic performing rights had become protected by further legislation. The *Fine Arts Copyright Act* was passed in 1862 and brought paintings, drawings and photographs within the realm of copyright which protected intellectual property for the life of the author plus seven years.

The *Copyright Act 1911* extended copyright to the typographical format of published editions. This Act was replaced by the *Copyright Act 1956* which, in turn, was superseded by the *Copyright, Designs and Patents Act 1988*. For the sake of brevity, the latter will hereafter be referred to as the CDPA.

Prior to these Acts, however, there had been a number of decided cases in which the concepts of an individual's labour and creation were upheld. One of the main concepts of copyright has been that of originality, and in 1890 there was a landmark judgment in the case of *Palgrave's Golden Treasury of Verse*, a compendium of poetry gathered together from the work of many poets, first published in 1861 and updated and published constantly since that date.

The *Golden Treasury* had been protected by compilation copyright and the issue before the court was that of originality. The court held:

"In cases of work not original in the proper sense of the term but composed of, or compiled or prepared from materials which are open to all, the fact that one man has produced such a work does not take away from anyone else the right to produce another work of the same kind and in doing so use all the materials open to him."

Defining a photograph

It is worth noting at this stage that Section 4(1)(a) of the CDPA defines an "artistic work" as, among other things, "a graphic work, photograph, sculpture or collage, irrespective of artistic quality". Section 4(2) says:

"Photograph means a recording of light or other radiation on any medium on which an image is produced or from which an image may by any means be produced, and which is not part of a film."

This is a rather more precise definition that that which was to be found in the 1956 Act, which was generally considered to be unsatisfactory as far as photographers were concerned.

A Government appointed committee under Mr Justice Whitford was set up in 1973 "to consider and report whether any, and if so what, changes are desirable in the law relating to copyright as provided in particular by the Copyright Act 1956." In representations to the committee, photographic bodies expressed the view that the definition of a photograph should be amended to exclude reprography, on the basis that photocopies produced automatically by a machine were not original but the result of a mechanical process and did not warrant copyright protection as photographs.

The current definition may or may not meet these objections. Photocopying machines, which are becoming more and more sophisticated, do, of course, make copies on paper by means of the transmission or recording of light on paper.

It is also worth noting that the phrase "irrespective of artistic quality", which was in the 1956 Act, is repeated in the CDPA. This is an important phrase, because a photograph can be appalling, it can be out of focus, over or under exposed and have no artistic merit whatsoever, yet still be protected by copyright. This underlines the basic theory of copyright, the protection of a person's creation – however poor that creation may be.

It was because of this that the Whitford Committee, when it reported in 1977, commented on the suggestion of photographic bodies as far as reprography was concerned, that this would introduce a standard of artistic merit which would be a new departure in copyright law and which, if carried further, might have implications in other fields.

The Whitford Committee also turned down a suggestion that the definition of a photograph should no longer exclude a cinemato-graph film, a distinction first introduced in the 1956 Act – the com-mittee could see no reason for putting back the clock.

This view has obviously been underlined in the CDPA even though the word "cinematograph" has been dropped. The use of the word film in the definition under the CDPA must be taken to refer to a cinematographic film or a videotape.

The scope of copyright

So what is, and is not, subject to copyright? The definition of a pho-tograph has already been stated, but because photographers so often photograph inanimate objects they ought to know what other works may be covered by copyright.

Section 4(1)(b) and (c) of the CDPA includes in the definition of artistic work a work of architecture, being a building or a model for a building, or a work of "artistic craftsmanship". Unfortunately this lat-ter phrase is not defined in the CDPA, but Section 4(2) helps by stat-ing that graphic work includes any painting, drawing, diagram, map, chart or plan and any engraving, etching, lithograph, woodcut or sim-ilar work. This, it is suggested, is a formidable list with practically no item of "artistic craftsmanship" omitted. Sculpture is deemed to include a cast or model made for the purpose of a sculpture.

It is interesting to note that the Act does not define collage, which is described in the *Concise Oxford Dictionary* as an abstract form of art in which photographs, pieces of paper, matchsticks, etc., are placed in juxtaposition and glued to the pictorial surface. It may be argued that as far as the CDPA is concerned a collage, like beauty, is in the eye of the beholder!

It is important for photographers to realise the extent to which copyright applies to visual objects, for so many photographs are taken of inanimate objects and artistic works and in many cases the pho-tographer is in ignorance of the copyright situation. Therefore, for the sake of clarity, what can best be described as "other people's copy-right" will be considered before the issue of photographic copyright.

Permitted acts

The CDPA sets out what can be done in relation to copyright works without an infringement of copyright occurring. Section 31(1) states that copyright in a work is not infringed by its "incidental inclusion" in, *inter alia*, an artistic work, film or cable programme.

(Since the Act was passed in 1988 there has been an explosion in the means of delivering pictures through a television set by means of satellite TV channels and through computers by means of the Internet. This could create an interesting situation if a user of the Internet or a satellite broadcaster was to be in breach of copyright. Would there be no breach under the Act because these two new channels of communication are not specifically mentioned in Section 31(1)? It is suggested that the use of film would be sufficient to bring a satellite channel within the ambit of the Act – always assuming that the broadcaster had offices within the jurisdiction of the Act – but the Internet could well be a different matter.)

A photographer taking a general shot which might have a copyright object in the background is unlikely to fall foul of copyright law, because the inclusion of such material would no doubt be held to be incidental. But what of a photographer who makes a collage of, say, photographs of famous models and then photographs and publishes the finished result? It can hardly be argued in any sense that the inclusion of those photographs is incidental.

Copyright in an artistic work is also not infringed by it being copied in the course of instruction or of preparation for instruction, providing that the copying is done by a person giving or receiving instruction and is not by means of a reprographic process.

Works on public display

Copyright which exists in buildings, models for buildings, sculptures and other works of artistic craftsmanship, is *not* infringed by photographing them when they are permanently situated in a public place or in premises open to the public.

This is the situation which obtained under the 1956 Act and is a commonsense point of view because, as we have seen, copyright exists to protect intellectual property and to allow the owner of such copyright to exploit it. The taking of photographs of buildings and works in a public place is not going to prevent the architect or designer from exploiting his work.

The Whitford Committee was critical of the phrase "premises open to the public" because they considered it to be of uncertain meaning. Nevertheless, the phrase is repeated in Section 62(1)(b) of the CDPA.

Consequently, pieces of sculpture and works of artistic craftsmanship on temporary display in public galleries may well be protected by copyright, but Section 62 of the CDPA does allow what might otherwise be considered breaches of copyright such as photography for private use.

As far as architecture is concerned, copyright in plans and drawings, or in models for a building, belongs to the architect unless he is employed, in which case, as in other cases of artistic work by an employed person, the copyright belongs to the employer unless there is an agreement to the contrary.

Such copyright used to run for 50 years from the death of the architect but now, for reasons which will be dealt with later in this chapter, runs for 70 years after death.

Section 62 of the CDPA states that copyright in a building is not infringed if it is painted, drawn, photographed or filmed.

Paintings and drawings

With paintings and drawings, copyright belongs to the artist and now continues for 70 years after death. The artist keeps the copyright even if the picture has been commissioned and it cannot be reproduced without the artist's permission.

Engravings, etchings, lithographs, woodcuts or similar works are also protected by copyright which belongs to the creator (or employer) so photographs of these subjects should not be taken without the consent of the copyright holder. Consent is only likely to be withheld if the photographs are being taken for commercial purposes.

Old masters would, of course, be out of copyright, and while these can be freely photographed, the problem for photographers is one of either gaining access to them or obtaining permission to take pictures of them from current owners. This and closely related topics will be discussed later in the book in the chapter dealing with confidentiality, privacy and trespass.

Everyday objects and handicrafts

There are a host of everyday objects which a photographer, for a variety of reasons, may wish to capture on film. Many of these objects may well be taken for granted, but may be subject to the provisions of the CDPA.

Part III of the Act states that a design right is a property right which exists in the design of any shape or configuration of the whole or part of an article. Under Part IV of the Act designs, which are registrable, mean features of shape, configuration, pattern or ornament applied by any industrial process, and which are of "aesthetic value".

Although copyright would be unlikely to exist in a can or bottle, the design for such may be registrable under the Act. An original design continues to be protected for 15 years from the end of the calendar year in which it was first recorded in a design document or an article was first made to the design, whichever first occurred.

On the other hand items of gold and silverware, jewellery, fabric, glassware, porcelain and pottery are all subject to copyright and would be protected for a period of 70 years as a work of artistic copyright.

A photographer taking pictures of such items might be held to be in breach of copyright, especially if the photographs were used for commercial purposes, but most photographs of mass produced articles are unlikely to produce copyright problems.

A photographer wishing to take photographs of an item of artistic craftsmanship should make basic inquiries about its provenance. If this leads to the photographer discovering the article is subject to copyright and he still wishes to capture it on film – especially if it is for commercial use – he should take the elementary precaution of seeking the consent of the copyright owner.

Common sense would seem to dictate that consent is unlikely to be refused. A photograph taken for commercial use is, in many cases, likely to increase the demand for the particular item or ones similar to it. As one of the objects of copyright law is to protect the intellectual or artistic work of the creator and enable the work to be exploited commercially, it would be ironic if permission was refused.

Entertainment and performances

There are other areas of copyright which may result in legal problems, which can be dealt with under the heading of entertainment.

It is not uncommon for newspapers and magazines to publish photographs taken from a television screen. This is a breach of copyright, but usually the television company concerned is quite happy to permit such material to be used provided an acknowledgement as to its source is printed alongside the pictures.

Stage shows, operas, ballets, concerts and other artistic performances are also protected by copyright, which exists not only in the script and/or music but also in stage and costume design, lighting and the production as a whole. But where photography is concerned it is only necessary to look at copyright as far as it affects capturing – on a still photograph – extracts from a performance. One photograph is unlikely to be considered to be a breach of copyright.

Crown and other exceptional copyrights

To use the words of the 1988 Act, when a work is "made by Her Majesty", or any servant or officer employed by the Crown and in the course of their work, if the work is of the type which would attract copyright protection, copyright will invest in the Crown.

The mind boggles at the thought of either the Queen or her civil servants writing and/or composing artistic, literary, dramatic or musical works – although Henry VIII is reputed to have written a number of songs including "Greensleeves". But if this should be the case, under the 1988 Act Crown copyright lasts for 125 years from the end of the calendar year in which it was written and/or composed. If on the other hand the work should be published commercially within 75 years of its composition, copyright would then last for 50 years from the end of the year in which it was published.

Copyright in Acts of Parliament as well as measures enacted by the General Synod of the Church of England lasts for 50 years from the end of the year in which the Royal Assent was given. All Acts of Parliament are published by Her Majesty's Stationery Office and are covered by Crown copyright. Publications by certain international organisations which would not normally enjoy the protection of UK copyright laws, also have similar protection.

The 1988 Copyright Act also granted to the Trustees for the Hospital for Sick Children, Great Ormond Street, London, the copyright in perpetuity of Sir James Barrie's play Peter Pan. The copyright has been left to the hospital by the author and would have expired under the new limits of time on 31st December 2007.

Finally, a curious anomaly was finally laid to rest by the 1988 Act. The Copyright Act of 1775 had conferred on universities and colleges perpetual copyright for their publications. This perpetual copyright will now cease to exist after 31st December 2039.

Exceptions to copyright

As can be seen from the above, it can be said that copyright exists in almost anything that has been produced as a result of a person's skill, labour and judgment. There is even copyright in a football fixture list which, though hardly a literary work, is a result of the skill and labour on the part of the compiler.

But there are exceptions to copyright: there is no copyright in an idea, or in news. Consequently any item in the news or something which would fall into the category of current affairs can be photographed without fear of breaching copyright. Nevertheless, copyright does exist in a photograph of an event which is newsworthy. So too would copyright exist in a written news report, because the protection granted by copyright is for the pictures and words describing or reporting the news, not the news itself.

As there is no copyright in ideas, there is nothing to stop a photographer from hiring a model used by Patrick Lichfield or David Bailey and using the same pose and location to create a picture similar to one taken by one of these leading figures. Although the photographer would rightly be guilty of plagiarism, he has used his own skill and labour in producing the photograph.

However, the situation would be very different if the photographer tried to pass off the photograph as having been taken by Lichfield or Bailey.

Although there is no copyright in ideas copyright does protect a person's original work, and it is worth briefly noting what is meant by "original". In *Kilvington Brothers Limited v Goldberg (1957)*, Mr Justice Judson held that novelty and inventiveness were not necessarily the test of originality. He held – though it must be remembered that the case he was trying concerned the design of a tombstone and not a photograph or any other artistic work – that to be original it must be the original expression of the thoughts of its creator. Although the case was a Canadian one, there is no doubt that it would be persuasive in a court of law in England and Wales.

On the surface, the judgment in this case may well seem to contradict the statement that there is no copyright in ideas, but the crucial question is that of the skill and labour involved.

So how would this apply to the imitation of a Lichfield or Bailey photograph? Again, the acid test is the question of skill and labour, and those criteria would be met by the photographer hiring the model and seeking out the same location, as well as posing the model in the same way, arranging any lighting that may be required, and physically taking the photograph.

Furthermore, it might be difficult to adjudicate on whether or not the same idea may have been conceived by one photographer at the same time as it was by another, or even a third.

The 1988 Act conferred for the first time copyright in speeches, but provided a speaker does not ban the speech from being reported, there is no copyright in that report except insofar as it belongs to the person or media which is reporting it.

People

No person has copyright in their own appearance. Anyone in a public place, or who can be seen from a public place, cannot legally object if their photograph is taken. Nevertheless there is always the risk of using such a photograph in such a way that it could be libellous.

A further word of caution is worthwhile: although there is nothing to stop a photographer taking anyone's photograph, as will be made clear in a later chapter the photographer could be guilty of a nuisance or harassment (although much would depend upon the circumstances of the individual case).

There are peoples in some parts of the world who shun having their photographs taken as they fear that the taking of the photograph will spirit away their soul thus precluding them from enjoying whatever life after death their religion promises them. Less than ten years ago while on holiday in West Africa, the author discovered that despite the fact they were devout Muslims, there are still some West Africans who will buy a ju-ju which they wear in the belief that it will prevent them from being photographed.

But even in the West photographers may encounter irrational and aggressive behaviour from people who object to being captured on film. Although in most countries there are no legal restrictions on taking photographs of people, photographers would be wise to exercise caution and respect the views of those who object.

The question of model release forms is dealt with in chapter 2.

Some recent changes

One very important change in the 1988 Act was that copyright in a photograph no longer expired, as was the case under the 1956 Act, 50 years after first publication, but at the end of the period of 50 years from the end of the calendar year in which the author died.

This remained the case until 1st January 1996, when legislation came into effect which implemented a European Union directive extending copyright protection to literary, dramatic, music and artistic works for the life of the author plus 70 years.

But not only did it extend copyright protection for items already enjoying protection, it revived protection for works for which copyright had expired in the United Kingdom before 31st December 1995, if they were still protected by the copyright laws of another European Economic Area state. This has been termed revived copyright.

This means that works – including photographs – by authors who died between 1925 and 1945 are now covered by revived copyright provided they were so protected within another European Economic Area state (which for most works would be the case in Germany). Dependent on the date of the death of the author, copyright may be extended for a period of between one year for a person who died in 1925 and twenty years for someone who died in 1945.

The new rules do *not* apply to Crown or Parliamentary copyright or to work generated by a computer.

These changes will be the cause of endless trouble for picture editors, who will now have to show even greater care in discovering whether a library picture is still in copyright, enjoys revived copyright, or is out of copyright.

Another problem which will have to be resolved is who will benefit by the revived copyright. If the photograph was taken by an employed person then in all probability copyright will belong to the employer. If the photograph was supplied by a freelance or someone who commissioned the photograph (and who under the 1956 Act held the copyright) then it is necessary to find, if at all possible, the current copyright holder.

The copyright holder may not be the original photographer or even the person who commissioned the photograph for, if the photograph had potential value, copyright could have been assigned by many methods to a third party.

On the 1st December 1996 Regulation 16 of the *Copyright and Related Rights Regulations* came into effect, which created the concept of "Publication Right". This right grants any person or organisation who holds photographs which have gone out of copyright and who for the first time publishes a previously unpublished photograph, a Publication Right for 25 years from the end of the year in which it is first published.

To qualify for this protection first publication must be in a country within the European Economic Area and the publisher of the work, at the time of first publication, must be a national of an EEA state. No such right will attach to publication of a work in which either Crown or Parliamentary copyright subsisted.

As the new regulations refer to publication after the expiry of copyright protection, it is possible to assume that this may not apply to works of unknown authorship – a concept introduced in the 1988 Act. The CDPA gives such works copyright protection for 50 years from the end of the calendar year in which the work(s) is first made available to the public. Unknown authorship only applies where not only is the author unknown, but it is also not possible to ascertain his identity by making "reasonable inquiries".

Today it is not uncommon for old photographic collections to be unearthed in attics, at boot sales, etc. Often these photographs are of historic and/or social significance and will inevitably find either a publisher or an exhibitor. Thus they can be of considerable value.

There are many famous old photographs which are out of copyright and have been so for many years, some of which have been compiled to demonstrate the development and history of photography, going back now for well over a century. The manner in which they are displayed in a book would be covered by compilation copyright, for even though the photographs are not original, the compiler has used skill and labour in the compilation.

As a result of the extension of copyright which has already been noted (but which does *not* apply to Crown and Parliamentary copyright) the position can be summarised as follows:

Photographs taken prior to the commencement of the CDPA will have their copyright extended by a further 20 years. But the beneficiary of the extension will not necessarily be the photographer for, if the photographer was commissioned, it is the person who commissioned the photograph who will hold the copyright unless he has assigned it to a third party or it has been assigned by operation of law such as in a will or bankruptcy.

Photographs taken after the CDPA came into force will remain in copyright for the life of the photographer plus 70 years, although again one must enter the *caveat* that the copyright may, for a number of reasons, be held by someone else.

Thus, as has been noted earlier in this section, this can, and in some circumstances undoubtedly will, cause enormous problems in determining who is the copyright owner.

2 Copyright for Photographers

Having examined the theory of copyright and those areas in which it exists as far as photographs are concerned, it is now necessary to look at who owns the copyright of photographs.

Section 1(1) of the CDPA states that copyright exists, *inter alia*, in artistic works which, as noted in the previous chapter, includes photographs.

Section 154(1) of the legislation states that work qualifies for copyright protection if the author was at the material time: (a) a British citizen, a British Dependent Territories citizen, a British National (Overseas), a British Overseas citizen, a British subject or a British protected person within the meaning of the British Nationality Act 1981; or (b) an individual domiciled or resident in the United Kingdom or another country to which relevant provisions of this part extend; or (c) a body incorporated under the law of a part of the United Kingdom or of another country to which the relevant provisions of this part extend.

The references "to which ...this part extends" means that Parliament may extend the provisions of copyright protection as far as publication in this country is concerned, to Commonwealth and foreign citizens and/or properly constituted companies which, in many cases, are likely to be signatories to international copyright conventions. By the same token, a photograph first published in a country to which this part of the Act extends would also have its copyright protected in this country. In fact, there are few parts of the world to which international conventions do not apply.

Photographers in employment

The CDPA made two radical changes as far as photographs were concerned, one of which affected employed photographers. Under the *Copyright Act 1956*, if a photographer was employed by the proprietor of a newspaper or similar periodical under a contract of service or apprenticeship, and a photograph was taken for publication in that periodical, copyright belonged to the proprietor "insofar as it relates to publication in any newspaper etc., or reproduction of the work for the purpose of it being published."

In all other respects the photographer was entitled to copyright remaining in the work.

Also under the 1956 Act – in the case of non-press work – where a photograph was taken in the course of a photographer's employment by another person, under a contract of service or apprenticeship, that other person was entitled to the copyright subsisting in the work.

Now, Section 11(2) of the CDPA states: "Where a literary, dramatic, musical or artistic work is made by an employee in the course of his employment, his employer is the first owner of the copyright in the work subject to any agreement to the contrary". It will be noted that this section does *not* have the subsidiary clause for press workers reserving copyright for other uses to the photographer.

The derogation of this right which was contained in the 1956 Act was vigorously challenged by such interested bodies as the National Union of Journalists and by many members of both Houses of Parliament, but to no avail. Now the only way in which a photographer can reserve to himself what might be called subsidiary rights, is if such an agreement is included in the contract of service.

Commissioned photography

The other major change in the law which came about in the CDPA was in commissioned photographs.

Prior to the CDPA, the person who commissioned the photograph was the owner of the copyright, and this was frequently a bone of contention. Photographers argued that it was the photographer who was responsible for the photograph and not the person who paid for it.

It was as a result of representations to the Whitford Committee that the CDPA altered the situation so that the photographer is now the copyright holder rather than the commissioner of the photograph.

It was also argued to the Whitford Committee that the person who actually operated the shutter of the camera was not necessarily the person whose artistic skill and expertise went into creating the photograph – such credit should go to the person responsible for organising the photography. Although the Whitford Committee felt such a definition lacked certainty, it nevertheless recommended that the author should be defined as the person responsible for the composition of the photograph.

Yet in the CDPA the only attempt to define authorship as far as photography is concerned is in Section 9(1) which says the author, in relation to a work, means the person who creates it.

This definition is itself open to criticism because, it is submitted, there is still a degree of uncertainty. For example, an advertising agency art director sketches out how he sees a particular advertisement. A photographer experienced in this particular type of photography is called in to translate the concept to finished product. The photographer uses his expertise to set up the photograph and it is the photographer who determines focus and shutter speed. Who can, with any certainty, say who was the creator of the photograph?

Nevertheless, there is no suggestion in the CDPA that the person commissioning the photograph will be the copyright holder.

However, cases such as *Williams v Settle (1960)* can still arise today. In this notable case a photographer was commissioned to take a photograph of the plaintiff's wedding. Two years later the plaintiff's father-in-law was murdered. The dead man appeared in the wedding photograph and the photographer sold copies to some national newspapers.

In the subsequent action it was held that copyright belonged to the plaintiff and not the photographer.

Williams v Settle will be mentioned again later in this chapter in the section dealing with moral rights. But in the context of copyright, the position in this case would have been different had the photographer taken the wedding pictures "on spec", even if he sold the pictures to the members of the wedding, as there would have been no commissioning of the photographs.

If a photographer does agree that the copyright should be the property of the person commissioning the work, he should consider a number of important factors and include them in the commissioning contract. Such contracts, in the interest of both parties, but especially the photographer, should be in writing.

At the time of the Whitford Committee, the Committee on Photographic Copyright which represented nine major organisations representing all aspects of photography, said the following points should be considered as important factors to be taken into account when considering what fee should be charged:

How will the photographs be reproduced/shown?
For what purpose will the work be reproduced?
How long (in time) will the work be reproduced/published/sold?
What is the print run – how many copies will be made?
In what geographical areas will the work be reproduced/published?
How many editions/impressions/versions are to be published?

These are points which any photographer considering assigning copyright to a commissioner should ask, for upon the answer must depend the size of the fee to be charged.

Ownership of originals

The CDPA did not answer one age-old question and source of much contention. That is: who owns the originals of commissioned photographs? For ownership is not always synonymous with copyright.

It had been the custom for many years for professional photographers to claim ownership of the negatives in the case of commissioned work. This claim is one I have never been happy with for, to the best of my knowledge, it had and has no foundation in law. Indeed, where a photographer charges the person commissioning the photograph for film(s) used, as well as developing and printing, I can see no legal grounds for the photographer refusing to hand over the negatives.

After all, the person commissioning the photograph has paid for the film and the developing of it. I see no reason why the application of chemicals to a film – for which the commissioner has paid – to change them into negatives, or transparencies, should give the photographer the right of ownership.

The only certain way round this is for photographers to ensure they buy their own film and do not charge the commissioner directly for it. The costs can simply be absorbed into the photographer's standard rates. Thereby the photographer retains ownership of the material and the subsequent negatives or slides.

In any event, under the CDPA, unless the photographer has assigned the copyright to the commissioner, the commissioner cannot make further use of the photographs for commercial purposes because the photographer owns the copyright.

Moral rights

As a result of the CDPA the concept of "moral rights" was introduced, which gives the photographer the right to be identified whenever his work is published commercially, or exhibited in public, or a visual image of it is broadcast or included in a cable programme service. It also covers the case where a film showing a visual image of the work is shown in public or copies of such a film are issued to the public.

However, Section 78 of the CDPA requires that the photographer must assert this right, to whoever it concerns, in writing. If the photographer fails to assert the right in this manner, he has no claim against a publisher who fails to give a credit.

Additionally, there are extensive exceptions to this moral right: when the photographer is employed and the photograph is taken as part of his employment; for any work made for the purpose of reporting current events, or where the work is published in a newspaper, magazine or similar periodical; or in an encyclopaedia, dictionary, yearbook or other collective work of reference and is made for, or made available with the consent of the author for, the purpose of such publication.

Nor does it apply to Crown or Parliamentary copyright or work in which copyright originally vested in an international organisation.

Moral rights are not assignable, but the right to be identified as the author of a photograph, or to object to derogatory treatment of the author's work, may be bequeathed in a will. In the event of the photographer dying intestate the moral right – which only applies to the author and not the copyright owner unless they are one and the same – continues to subsist until twenty years after a person's death and the right is exercisable by the photographer's personal representatives.

A person who has his moral rights infringed has a right to sue, for the breach of statutory duty, the person who has infringed these rights.

False attribution

Apart from the right to have their work acknowledged – except in those circumstances referred to above – Section 84 of the CDPA gives a photographer the right not to have work falsely attributed to him. This situation could arise if a photograph is published or exhibited with the name of a photographer who did not take the pictures given as the author.

Under Section 86(2) this right continues to subsist until 20 years after a person's death.

It is difficult to conceive of circumstances, other than for a fraudulent purpose, where the name of a leading photographer would be given as the author of a photograph he did not take, although of course there could be circumstances where a photographer is wrongly named by mistake. False attribution would also apply if anyone sought to possess or deal in a photograph in the course of business, using the name of a photographer who was not the author of them.

As far as "doctoring" or manipulating photographs is concerned, a photographer whose work has been treated in this manner may seek an injunction – which a court may grant if it considers it an adequate remedy in the circumstances – which will prohibit such treatment of the photograph unless a disclaimer is made, in such terms and in such manner as may be approved by the court, disassociating the photographer from this treatment.

Rights in private photographs

Section 85(1) of CDPA states that "a person who for private and domestic purposes commissions the taking of a photograph or making of a film..." has the right not to have (a) copies issued to the public; (b) copies exhibited or shown to the public; (c) copies broadcast or included in a cable programme.

Since this right applies to a photograph or film taken for "private or domestic purposes" it is obvious that a wedding group – or a similar function or party – would fall into this category. This section would therefore *not* make *Williams v Settle* irrelevant.

The section refers specifically to a photograph being issued, or exhibited or shown in public, thus raising a number of interesting points.

Would "shown in public" cover publication in a newspaper? A photograph published in a newspaper, if not within the meaning of "shown in public", must surely be covered by the term "issued to the public".

But there is a more intriguing point to be considered, especially by high street photographers who exhibit portfolios, portraits, etc, in shop windows. Common sense dictates that this too must come under the definition of exhibiting or showing in public, and it is reasonable to assume that inclusion of similar photographs in a promotional brochure would also be exhibiting to the public, albeit a restricted section.

As far as works held on computer and available to view via the Internet are concerned, in *R v Arnold (1996)* the Court of Appeal held that the availability of images to others via computer links does constitute an "act of publication".

Photographers may, however, look to protection offered by Section 87 of the CDPA, which does not make it unlawful to exhibit or display photographs take for private and domestic purposes if consent is given.

Wedding and portrait photographers in particular should bear this important point in mind when accepting a photographic commission. The most effective way photographers can ensure that problems do not arise is by getting the commissioner to waive their moral rights and to get such a waiver in writing. Such permission, unless a contrary intention is expressed, made in favour of the owner or prospective owner of the copyright, is presumed to extend to his licensees and successors.

Copyright notification

There are certain basic steps all photographers should take in protecting the copyright of their photographs.

In all cases each print or slide should bear, or have attached to it, the name and address (and/or telephone number) of the photographer prefaced by the statement "Copyright of...". It may also be useful to add the year in which the photograph was created.

Additionally, or as an alternative, one can use the internationally recognised copyright symbol: ©. Although there is no specific requirement (in the UK) for a photograph to bear this symbol it may be useful for it to do so since it is widely recognised, even where the English language may not be. See also the section below on international copyright conventions.

Copyright infringement

Even the mere copying of a photograph is what the Act describes as "an act restricted by copyright" unless the copier has the permission of the copyright holder. It is even a breach of copyright to include a photograph which is protected by copyright in a broadcast (television) or cable programme.

The CDPA deals in depth with what is described as secondary infringement of copyright and infringing copies. This can best be summed up as possessing in the course of a business, selling or offering for sale, letting or offering to let for hire, a work protected by copyright, or distributing the work otherwise than in the course of a business, to such an extent as to effect prejudicially the rights of the copyright owner.

On the other hand, "fair dealing" in a photographic work for the purpose of research or private study does not infringe copyright. However, the CDPA offers no explanation as to what would constitute fair, or indeed for that matter unfair, dealing.

Fair dealing with a work for the purpose of criticism or review would not infringe copyright providing this is accompanied by sufficient acknowledgement as to the identity of the copyright owner.

What, then, would be the position of a newspaper or magazine if it wished to review a collection of photographs and reproduce one or more as part of that review?

Quite distinct from fair dealing is the question of whether a substantial number are reproduced. It is only when the court has determined that a substantial number have been used that the question of whether or not this constitutes fair dealing arises.

Once this question has arisen the degree of substantiality – that is to say, the quantity and value of photographs used – becomes an important factor in determining whether there has been fair dealing. As in all aspects of the law, there can be no hard and fast rule: each case must depend on its own particular facts.

It should be noted that the use of a photograph for the reporting of current events is not fair dealing under Section 30(2) of the CDPA, although it is for other works. Although the use of other copyright works for the purpose of reporting current events is not an infringement if sufficient credit is given, in the case of photographs the copyright owner's permission must be sought.

Certain exceptions are also made for copyright work being copied for educational purposes, providing such copying is done by the person giving or receiving instruction and is not by means of a reprographic process.

Neither is copyright infringed by anything done for the purpose of Parliamentary or judicial proceedings or proceedings of a Royal Commission or a statutory inquiry.

Since publication of the previous edition of this book, there has been a virtual explosion of multi-media outlets such as cable, CD-ROM, the Internet, etc, in which copyright infringement may well be prevalent. This will be dealt with in greater detail in the next chapter, along with the often thorny problem of assignment of copyright.

Remedies for infringement

Infringement of copyright is actionable on the part of the copyright owner, to whom a number of remedies are open.

The copyright owner can seek damages, an injunction restraining future breaches of copyright, an account of profit made as a result of the copyright breach, or other remedy as would be available for the breach of any other property right.

Section 97 of the CDPA provides that in an action for infringement, if it is shown that at the time of the infringement the defendant did not know, and had no reason to believe, that copyright subsisted in the work, the plaintiff is not entitled to damages. Nevertheless, in such circumstances the plaintiff can still enforce any other remedy available to him.

In most minor cases of infringement a photographer can expect to receive damages that compensate for any financial loss resulting from the infringement. Usually this will be the sum that would have been payable had a licence to publish been granted in the normal way.

However, the CDPA also empowers a court, having regard to all the circumstances, and with particular reference to the flagrancy of the infringement and any other benefit received by the defendant as a result of the infringement, to award "such additional damages as the justice of the case may require."

An account of profit – which requires the defendant to pay the plaintiff any profits received as a result of the infringement – can be claimed as an alternative to damages, but not in addition.

Section 99 gives the copyright holder the right to order an offender to deliver up photographs that are in breach of copyright, while Section 111 provides for the forfeiture and destruction of offending material, with the right of the court to take into account the adequacy or otherwise of other available remedies.

Obviously it is to be hoped that a court would take into consideration the ability of a person in breach of copyright to actually pay any damages awarded if this is to be considered as an alternative to any forfeiture order.

Criminal liability

Most copyright offences are actionable under civil law. However, there is a criminal liability for making for sale or hire, importing into the United Kingdom other than for private or domestic use, or possessing in the course of a business with the view to committing an act infringing the copyright, a copy which is, and which the person knows or has reason to believe is, an infringing copy of a copyright work.

Section 107 also imposes criminal liability where there is a prejudicial effect on the copyright owner if a person distributes otherwise than in the course of business, an infringing article.

This section is unlikely to affect any but top photographers whose work might well be pirated and sold by unscrupulous people as an original.

International copyright

Finally, there is the question of international copyright conventions to be considered. In past years there have been a number of treaties between this country and other countries which provide copyright protection outside the British Isles. Of course, the reverse also applies, whereby the work of foreign nationals is protected within the UK.

There is the Berne Convention, which goes back to 1886 and has been the subject of a number of revisions, the last being in Paris in 1971. In the same year and in the same city the Universal Copyright Convention of 1952 was revised. The changes made in the Berne Convention were of a minor nature and have not yet been ratified in this country except for administrative clauses.

The difference between the Berne Convention and the Universal Copyright Convention is that the former USSR was a most important country which was party to the latter convention, but not the former.

Under the Universal Copyright Convention, copyright protection last for the life of the author plus 25 years. However, this is a minimum term.

One important fact to bear in mind is that in order to secure copyright protection in countries which are Universal Copyright Convention signatories, it is necessary for all work to bear the international copyright symbol (as discussed earlier) followed by the name of the copyright owner and the year in which the work is first published. However, this is not necessary for work first published in countries which subscribe to the Berne Convention.

As far as this country is concerned it is the revision to the Berne Convention in Stockholm in 1967 which is important, as this gave photographers the same protection in all countries which are signatories to the agreement as they have in the United Kingdom.

Obviously, being a member of the European Union, the United Kingdom will continue to observe changes in copyright laws which emanate from the EU. This has already happened, as we have seen, with the length of copyright being extended to the life of the author plus 70 years.

Model release forms

Although not within the scope of copyright law, this is perhaps an appropriate place to deal with the question of model release forms.

Strictly speaking, such forms are not necessary in law. As we have seen, there is no copyright in a person's features or body and copyright always belongs to the photographer, especially if he has paid a model.

The continued use of the term "release" is potentially misleading, since it implies that a subject must approve the release of photographs before they can be used. In fact these forms are no more than an agreement of terms between model and photographer, and a perhaps more accurate terminology for such documents would be "modelling agreement".

Be that as it may, model release forms serve a more than useful purpose as far as the use of photographs is concerned, in so far as they clarify and provide a record of the agreement between photographer and model.

Depending on the wording of the form, the photograph can be put to any legitimate use without the model having to be consulted, or having any comeback – unless, of course, an accompanying caption libels the model. The pictures can be used for publication in any form including advertising.

A model release form can also serve as a receipt and will obviate any dispute as to whether or not an agreed fee has been paid.

It is best for the release to be signed at the end of a modelling session as the model will then be perfectly aware of the type of photographs which have been taken. If a model under the age of 18 has been used, the form should be counter-signed by a parent or guardian.

If the model works through an agency the agency can sign on the model's behalf, and this will be as legally binding as if the model had signed the release personally. However, it is interesting to note that the Association of Model Agents no longer recommends the use of model release forms, and many model agencies simply incorporate details of agreed use and payment into their standard booking forms.

It should be noted that although release forms are valuable for the above reasons and should always be used wherever possible, a model's refusal to sign at the end of a session does not necessarily mean the photographer is unable to make use of the photographs.

Unless copyright has been passed to the model, the model has no legal grounds for preventing subsequent publication of the photographs, whether a release has been signed or not. However, if a photographer has promised a model not to publish, but subsequently does so, the model may be able to sue for breach of contract or breach of confidence.

Although a photographer is at liberty to take photographs of the public at large, it can be useful to get release forms signed where one or more people appear prominently in a picture. This is particularly the case if the pictures are subsequently placed with a picture agency that may sell rights for advertising use or for travel brochures and similar publicity material. Most picture agencies, and some publishers, require that releases be available for such pictures.

Release forms, or at least some other form of written permission, may also be useful if people are photographed in the street for a feature article for a newspaper, magazine or broadcast, as opposed to news purposes. Of course a feature may or may not be construed as "news" or "current events"; much would depend on the subject matter and contents. A "vox pop" feature in which photographs of people who are expressing their views are used, would in all probability fall into the category of current events, since the object of such an exercise on the part of the media is to elicit views on an item of topical interest.

3 Copyright Assignment and Licensing

Some photographs have great value, and this is where copyright protection and the rights of a copyright holder cease to be an intangible theory but become a valuable commodity.

A freelance or amateur photographer who is fortunate enough to be able to capture a dramatic incident should be careful of any agreement he signs with a newspaper, magazine, television/cable company or any picture-gathering organisation. The potential purchaser may well be prepared to pay a substantial sum for a dramatic and exclusive picture, but will almost inevitably want to purchase the copyright outright or have exclusive rights for, say, syndication or overseas use.

The obvious reason for this is that it gives the purchaser the opportunity of recouping money paid for the images. The photographer who finds himself in this position should therefore read carefully any agreement he signs and be absolutely certain what rights he may be signing away and for how long.

To give some indication of the position, the magazine *Practical Photography* once asked what the *Daily Mirror* would offer for a hypothetical picture of someone diving into the Thames to save a Royal corgi from drowning while the Queen looked on aghast. After getting over his amusement the then deputy picture editor of the *Mirror* told the magazine:

"Well first of all I'd want to make damn sure that he hadn't already offered it to any other paper. It's quite a common practice for photographers to try auctioning a picture by phoning one or two of the other national newspapers and then phoning us saying 'so-and-so offered so much' hoping we'll make a better offer.

"No, if it was a really good picture, sharp with clear faces and well composed, I'd get a team and editor down right away. You have to have an editor for negotiations if a picture's likely to be worth more than £2,000, and we would want to make very sure that the photographer had copyright.

"I'd say we would start talking at around £5,000 to £10,000 for that hypothetical picture. Then you'd have to come to some agreement about world syndication rights. This is usually worked on a 60/40 percentage basis with the 60 going to the photographer.

"But if he was prepared to sell us the rights they would probably be worth another £10,000 or so. It depends on a whole number of factors really."

Bearing in mind that the hypothetical payment figures referred to were quoted some years ago, this summarises the type of deal a photographer could make with a world-beating photograph. If the photographer owns the copyright, what he receives for the picture is based on current worth and how shrewdly he can bargain. It is during the bargaining process that the photographer must reach a decision about how much he wants and what rights he is going to assign to the particular party with whom he is bargaining.

In an ideal world the photographer would be well advised to seek legal advice, but when the worth of a photograph so often depends on its topicality and time is of the essence, this is a counsel of perfection. But it is no use a disgruntled photographer complaining after the event that he signed away all or some of his rights for, unless fraud or duress was involved, the law will not intervene.

Rights licensing

As can be seen, copyright may be and often is a valuable commodity which can be sold either wholly or in part. It can also be given away either as a gift or by bequeathing it in a will, in which case whoever acquires the copyright takes over all the rights which had accrued to the previous copyright holder.

Copyright is a property right the licensing of which can be subdivided into three main areas:

1. As to the nature of the right; for example, film rights, publishing rights, broadcasting rights, etc.
2. As to the territory where the rights will apply; for example,

Britain, Europe, the Commonwealth or worldwide.

3. The period of time for which the right is assigned (which can be for no more than the lifetime of the photographer plus 70 years).

For example, this means that a photographer can assign rights in a photograph for publication in the USA for a period of 10 years, at the end of which time the US rights revert back to him. At the same time he can retain the rights for the UK while selling them for five years in Europe and twenty years for the rest of the world outside the USA and Europe. In other words, copyright can be sliced in many ways for the benefit of the owner!

Assignment of copyright

Assignment of copyright has to be in writing – preferably, as has already been noted, in a deed of assignment drawn up by a lawyer – or by operation of law. Operation of law means, as mentioned above, leaving it in a will to a particular person, persons or body. If the photographer died intestate, copyright would pass to whoever was entitled to it under the law governing intestacy.

For a copyright holder who is unfortunate enough to become bankrupt, copyright would vest in the receiver for the benefit of creditors. Similarly, any body corporate which goes into liquidation would find any copyright it held and which had a monetary value would almost certainly be sold to reduce debts.

Some years ago it was not unknown for some publishers to accept a photograph for publication and when paying for its use endorse the back of the cheque with the following, or similar words: "Cashing this cheque will be taken as passing the copyright in the photograph for which this cheque is payment to...", with the name of the publishing company inserted.

This was never a valid method of acquiring copyright and the practice is all but dead, but it has been replaced (or perhaps it would be correct to say that publishers have sought to replace it) with something far more restrictive.

Publishing agreements

That publishers, especially in the magazine and newspaper field, have sought to introduce restrictive contracts for paying for photography, is due in no small part to the fact that what was once a fragmented industry has by mergers, amalgamations and acquisitions become restricted to a few major corporations controlling the bulk of titles published.

As so often happens in what is a near monopolistic situation, many of these major publishing houses have sought to introduce restrictive contracts as far as freelance contributors are concerned. While doing research for this edition of *The Photographer & the Law*, the author has had the opportunity to examine many agreements in which large publishing houses have sought to use their financial clout and dominant position to the disadvantage of the photographer.

These publishers have been trying to impose "all rights" contracts on contributors, be they photographers, writers, illustrators and, in all probability, cartoonists. Not only have they tried to get all rights, they have also required the contributor to indemnify the publisher against any legal claim, when the standard practice has for many years been for the publisher to accept joint responsibility with the contributor.

One of the reasons for this has been the explosion of multi-media sources, with publishers not only publishing magazines and newspapers but also reproducing material on the Internet and on CD-ROM. Newspapers also have financial interests in national, regional and local television and cable companies as well as radio.

One major publisher sought to impose on contributors an agreement giving the publisher the rights to re-publish information (presumably including photographs) in electronic media. This company acknowledged that it was necessary under law to receive the contributor's consent for reuse, and this was to be obtained by the contributor signing a commissioning agreement assigning copyright and other worldwide rights. The contributor was also expected to waive the benefit of all his moral rights. Payment would only be made on receipt of the signed form.

Some publishers have sought to get photographers to sign away copyright not only in the work in question, but in both past and future work which the photographer had done or might do for a particular magazine.

One major organisation wanted further warranties; for the contributor to warrant that the authors of any copyright material contained in the work have waived all their existing rights and any other moral rights which may be enacted in the future. This means, of course, that the contributor has the responsibility of ensuring that anyone with only the remotest interest in the work signs away their rights, now and in the future.

Needless to say these far-reaching contracts have been challenged by photographers' associations, trade unions and other bodies whose members are likely to be affected. As a result many of these demands, which some may call outrageous, have been withdrawn.

But if a photographer should be asked to sign a contract with a particular publisher and/or magazine – for it seems to be mainly magazines seeking to introduce such agreements – the photographer is not obliged to part with copyright in past photographs which have been published unless offered reasonable payment. And if the contractual agreement is that in present and future work copyright passes to the publisher, and the photographer has to waive moral rights, then the photographer should seek to increase his fees substantially for this work.

It must be remembered that if the photographer is a specialist in a particular field and has a reputation for his abilities in that field, he may well have the upper hand and be able to demand variation of these terms. Furthermore, as will have been noted by the earlier reference to the picture offered to the *Daily Mirror*, in many other instances the photographer may be in a strong bargaining position.

The new media

One major difficulty photographers will increasingly face is in protecting their copyright as far as multi-media outlets such as CD-ROMs and the Internet are concerned. This leads to the question of how to protect copyright from piracy in this particular section of the media.

With digital imaging, a portion of a photograph can be extracted and, with the aid of the electronic media techniques now available, be used in a collage or mixed with other images. Whether or not that would constitute an infringement would depend on whether or not a court thought such infringement was substantial. There is no yardstick of what is or is not substantial; that, like beauty, is in the eye of the beholder. The ease with which those skilled in the use of computers can gain illegal entry – hack into – a computer means that electronically stored photographs can easily be transferred to a disc or published on the Internet.

However, under the *Computer Misuse Act 1990* it is, *inter alia*, an offence to hack into a computer in furtherance of some other crime, and it is to be remembered that in certain cases breaches of the CDPA do carry penal sanctions. Therefore there is a strong probability that a court might hold that illegal and unauthorised use of a photograph obtained by hacking into a computer, constituted "some other crime."

The 'Potawatamie Indian' case

In September 1996 there was what could prove to be a groundbreaking judicial decision in the Ontario Court of Justice. The London-based picture agency Tony Stone Images won a case against a Canadian designer, which is likely to set a precedent for the rights of photographers when it comes to image manipulation.

In 1994 the designer won a major design contest with an entry the focal point of which was a direct copy of a photographic portrait created by photographer Nick Vedros. The image, called "Potawatamie Indian", had been licensed to Tony Stone Images. The designer did not deny that he had copied the photograph, but claimed there had been no infringement of copyright as the image was transferred from one medium to another, from a photograph to a drawing.

In its judgment the court confirmed that copyright remained with the original photographer regardless of the medium, even when transferred to an electronic medium.

This decision may well have far-reaching repercussions in those countries where the English common law system operates. In England and Wales, the decision of the Canadian court would be regarded by judges as persuasive. In all probability it would be endorsed, so bringing the court decision into English case law where it would become a binding precedent.

Photographic competitions

Photographic competitions are popular and high standards of photographic initiative, imagination and quality are revealed as a result of such competitions.

Any photographer entering such a competition must, for his own protection, first read and understand the rules of the competition.

To begin with, many of them state that entries will only be returned if stamped addressed envelopes are sent with photographs or transparencies.

Also among the conditions may be acceptance of a disclaimer by the organiser of the competition, absolving them from liability for loss of, or damage to, the photographs. Thus the photographer is on notice that if there is loss or damage, he has no claim against the organiser, for he has accepted the risk.

Such competitions frequently have as a condition that prize-winning entries may be used for publication, promotional or advertising purposes, or even that copyright passes to the promoter or publication concerned. By signing such an entry form, which is more than likely to state that the entrant has read and agreed to be bound by the conditions of entry, one is, in effect, assigning copyright. The photographer must therefore consider whether or not the prizes on offer are worth the loss of copyright.

One must take a common sense point of view and ask this question: "If my entry is of a sufficiently high standard to win a prize, could I benefit more if I did not enter the competition, retained my copyright, and tried to get higher rewards by selling it elsewhere?"

The answer may be "no", for competitions which offer good prizes may be based on a subject or theme in which only the promoter has an interest, and entering the competition may be the only chance the photographer has of realising the value of a particular photograph.

But to be avoided are those competitions – which happily are becoming fewer these days – where the rules state that the copyright in *all* entries passes to the organisers. By this method the organisers are obtaining the copyrights in perhaps hundreds of original pictures, yet only a select handful will receive any prizes. The vast majority will have given away their copyright for nothing.

Photo agency contracts

Gifted amateur photographers as well as professionals frequently lodge the results of their work with photo agencies, which in turn provide photographs to newspapers, magazines, advertising agencies or anyone requiring a particular picture. For many photographers this is a useful way of making money from their photographs without the trouble of having to seek outlets themselves, especially if they have extensive coverage of a particular subject or geographical area.

These agencies do a good job, but it must be remembered that their primary aim is to make money for themselves, not just the photographer. Photographers placing work with such an agency will usually be asked to sign a formal contract containing various terms and conditions. It is essential for the photographer to understand the terms and conditions of any agreement he enters into with an agency, especially in regard to questions of copyright and copyright acknowledgement.

Copyright duration

In this and the preceding two chapters various references have been made to the duration of copyright, and it may be of help to photographers if they have the following thumbnail guide:

For photographs taken after the CDPA came into force on 1st August 1989, copyright lasts now for 70 years from the end of the year in which the photographer dies. (But where the work has been generated by a computer it expires at the end of 50 years from the end of the year in which the work was made.) The copyright is owned by the photographer unless he is employed when, unless there is an agreement to the contrary, it is owned by his employer.

For photographs taken before 31st July 1989 and after 1st June 1957, copyright would normally have expired 50 calendar years from the end of the year of first publication – but this has now been extended to 70 years.

Other and more esoteric forms of copyright involving the state and international organisations, which most photographers are unlikely to come up against, have been dealt with in Chapter 1.

4   Libel

It is frequently said that the camera cannot lie: as far as this refers to the capturing on film of a person, object or incident, it is undoubtedly true. However, photographs in conjunction with captions have been, and will probably continue to be, the subject of libel actions.

Since the first edition of this book was published in 1984, developments in electronic and digital imaging have made it child's play to alter photographs. Some examples which have been published in recent years could well have been the subject of a libel action if the "victim" of the doctored photograph had thought fit to bring an action.

But before discussing doctoring further, it is necessary to look at libel, which is part of the law of defamation which exists to protect the professional and private – that is moral – reputation of a person from an unjustified attack.

Defamation covers both the spoken and written word. The spoken word, slander, can be conveniently omitted here because a photograph is classified with the written word as being in permanent form, whereas the spoken word is transient. However, untrue oral statements made on television or radio are classified as libellous rather than slanderous as is, under the *Theatres Act 1968*, a public performance of a play.

To succeed in a libel action the plaintiff must prove three points:
1. The words refer to the plaintiff.
2. They were published in permanent form.
3. They were defamatory or capable of bearing a defamatory meaning.

Definitions

So what is defamatory? Unfortunately there is no all-embracing definition of defamation as far as the law is concerned. What may be defamatory today may not be considered to be so twenty years hence.

Not many years ago to describe someone as "gay" meant that that person was, to quote a dictionary definition: "lively, merry, light-hearted, cheerful, bright..." Today it would be necessary add something like: "contemporary expression for someone who is homosexual."

Although to describe a person as light-hearted, smiling and bright would in no way be thought of as being defamatory, would it be defamatory to call a heterosexual "gay"? Would a judge consider it to be capable of bearing a defamatory meaning, and would a jury hold that in the context in which the word was used and, perhaps more important, in today's climate, that it was in fact defamatory?

The first satisfactory definition of what is defamatory was that of Baron Parke, in *Parminter v Copeland (1840)*, who held that a publication calculated to injure the reputation of another by exposing him to "hatred, ridicule or contempt" was defamatory.

Many years later – 84 to be exact – the deficiency of this definition was recognised when in *Tournier v National Provincial and Union Bank of England*, Lord Justice Atkin observed: "...but it is obvious that suggestions might be made very injurious to a man's character in business which would not, in the ordinary sense, incite hatred, ridicule or contempt; for example an imputation of a clever fraud which, however much to be condemned morally and legally, might not yet excite what a member of a jury might understand as hatred or contempt."

Next came a further definition which, at first sight, seems strange. In the last days of the Czarist Empire in Russia, the monk Rasputin rose to prominence in the court. In the early 1930s, after the death of Rasputin and many of the Czar's family, MGM Pictures made a film in which it was suggested that Princess Youssoupoff had been either seduced or raped by Rasputin.

The Princess, then living in exile in Paris, sued for libel. MGM were unable to prove that she had, in fact, been either seduced or ravished by Rasputin. Now it would appear that to have been seduced or, particularly, raped, is unlikely to expose a person to hatred, ridicule or contempt, but Lord Justice Slessor in the Court of Appeal made the following points:

"...as has been frequently pointed out in libel, not only is the matter defamatory if it brings the plaintiff into hatred, ridicule or contempt by reason of some moral discredit on her part, but also if it tends to make the plaintiff be shunned and avoided without moral discredit on her part."

It seems strange today to think that a woman said to have been seduced or raped by anyone, let alone a thorough scoundrel as Rasputin undoubtedly was, should be shunned or avoided, but this is a fine example of how reactions change over the years.

However, today, to falsely allege that someone has AIDS, or of even being HIV positive, might well cause people with little or no idea of how such a condition can be passed to another, to shun or avoid the person against whom the allegation is made.

In a changing and uncertain world one thing is certain, and that is that the law does not stand still. It is constantly changing and finding remedies for injuries for which no remedies existed hitherto. Libel is no exception, so it is not surprising to find the definition of what is defamatory extended yet again, this time in the case of *Sim v Stretch (1936)*.

It was again Lord Atkin, by this time a Lord of Appeal in Ordinary, in a House of Lords judgment, who was critical of the definition of Baron Parke, and a further test was evolved: would the words complained of tend to lower the plaintiff in the estimation of right-thinking members of society?

Over the years there have been a number of libel actions which were brought because of allegations which had been made about the competence or otherwise of a particular person. This has led to what can be called an omnibus definition: that the words complained of disparaged the person in his office, profession or trade.

Thus we now have four definitions of what constitutes a defamatory statement. They are a statement or statements which:

1. Expose a person to hatred, ridicule or contempt.
2. Cause him to be shunned or avoided.
3. Lower him in the estimation of right-thinking members of society generally.
4. Disparage him in his office, trade or profession.

Candid camera shots may also present a risk of an action for libel, as by their very definition such photographs are often only successful if they depict people in amusing (to others), embarrassing, and often humiliating, situations. Great care should be taken with the use of such photographs, and if at all possible consent to publication agreed in writing by the persons involved.

Conditions for libel

As has already been noted, what can be held to be defamatory can change over the years. Generally, most libel cases are heard by a judge and jury. It is for the judge to hold if the words complained of are capable of bearing a defamatory meaning, and for the jury to decide whether or not they were, in fact, defamatory. If the judge decides the words are not capable of bearing a defamatory meaning, that is the end of the case.

To succeed in a libel action the plaintiff has to prove not only that the words were defamatory, but that they were published and referred to him. As far as books, newspapers and magazines are concerned, publication is presumed.

As there must be publication to a third person for the tort of libel to be complete, there can be no libel if the offending and obviously libellous material is published only to the person libelled. Such would be the case if a letter or a photograph which could be construed as libellous is sent to the subject of the libel (although the question of criminal libel – which is dealt with later in this chapter – may arise).

If that person chooses to show the libellous material to a third party he cannot claim that he has been libelled by the originator of the material, as he (the offended person) was responsible for the publication himself.

However there is no doubt – and it must never be forgotten – that a photograph which because of either its caption or because it has been doctored or manipulated so that it is libellous, would in fact be libellous if published to a third person.

This raises an interesting point for photographers: if negatives of potentially libellous photographs are handed to a commercial firm for developing and printing, could this be held to constitute publishing?

There is no doubt that the handing in of a telegram or the posting of a postcard containing libellous material does constitute publication, as it will be seen by a third party. But whether or not handing negatives to a processing firm would be held to be publication is more difficult to judge. With the mechanical process used today it is possible for films to be developed and printed without them being seen by the human eye during any part of the process. On the other hand, it is often the custom for those operating the machinery to check prints for correct colour register and other technical purposes, and material seen in this way would undoubtedly constitute publication.

So, as has been noted before, the issue of publication would depend on the facts of an individual case and whether or not anyone had, in fact, looked at the offending material.

With the rapid growth of the Internet and the ease with which material contained on it can be downloaded by subscribers, placing or sending a potentially libellous photograph on it would, under *R v Arnold (1996)*, be held to be publication.

What is important is that the person claiming that he has been libelled has been either identified by name or, if unnamed, is capable of being identified by a person or persons known to him.

Innuendo

It is possible therefore, to have a situation where a photograph and caption can be libellous without the person portrayed being named. To understand why, it is necessary to look at the question of what libel lawyers refer to as the innuendo, a word which is derived from the Latin word meaning to nod to or hint at. It is frequently pleaded by plaintiffs when words complained of as being libellous are not defamatory in themselves. They become defamatory by reasons of their conjunction with another statement or because of some extrinsic circumstance or fact.

Two cases which illustrate the meaning of innuendo when linked with a photograph or illustration are *Cassidy v Daily Mirror (1929)* and *Tolley v Fry (1931)*.

In the first case a racehorse owner named Michael Cassidy was attending racing at Aintree accompanied by a lady. A *Daily Mirror* photographer took a photograph which was published with a caption based on information given by Cassidy. The caption read: "Mr Michael Cassidy and Miss..., whose engagement has been announced." Unfortunately for the newspaper, Cassidy was married, but separated from his wife who brought an action for libel.

She pleaded the innuendo in the caption, that those who knew her as Mrs Cassidy would think she was living a lie and that she was not in fact Cassidy's wife but his mistress with whom he had been living. Mrs Cassidy was awarded £500 damages.

Today such a situation would be covered by The *Defamation Act 1996*, which has in many respects amended the 1952 Act of the same name. Under the 1952 Act there would be a defence of unintentional defamation, when innocent publication could be claimed and this was accompanied by an offer of amends. This has been replaced with something similar; under the 1996 Act it is now necessary for a publication to show that, having taken reasonable care, there was no reason to believe that the statement referred to the aggrieved party or was likely to be understood to refer to him, or that the person publishing the statement had no reason to believe that it was false and defamatory of the aggrieved person. Such a defence, of course, would have to be accompanied by a published apology and offer of damages.

In determining whether the person responsible for publication did take reasonable care, regard has to be given to the extent of his responsibility for the content of the statement or the decision to publish it, the nature and circumstances of the publication, and the previous conduct or character of the author, editor or publisher.

This latter qualification could well mean that a publication which consistently used doctored or digitally altered photographs, or was careless with captions, might have this held against it.

In *Cassidy's* case there can be no doubt that had the above defence been available the newspaper would have paid a more modest sum and avoided litigation.

But would a similar defence have helped in Tolley's case, where the defendant was a well known chocolate manufacturer?

Tolley was a respected amateur golfer and Fry published in an advertisement a caricature of Tolley playing golf with a bar of Fry's chocolate sticking out of his pocket. It was accompanied by a limerick equating the quality of the chocolate with that of the playing ability of Tolley.

As an amateur and former amateur champion, Tolley claimed that the innuendo was that he had, for gain or reward, allowed his name and features to be used for advertising the chocolate. He was awarded £1,000 damages, though it was not until a final hearing in the House of Lords that the case was definitely settled in Tolley's favour.

It is arguable that as the offending caricature and accompanying words were in an advertisement, they would not have attracted either the old defence under the 1952 Act, or the new one contained in the Act of 1996.

Problems with locations

There are instances where careless use of photographs and/or locations have caused publishers problems.

Some years ago a well-known British glamour magazine published photographs of nude models posing on a moored motor launch. There was nothing obscene or exceptional about the photographs but, unfortunately for the magazine, the name of the motor launch was clearly visible. Its owner alleged that people who knew him from his boat would believe that he was in the habit of allowing nude girls to disport themselves on it. The case was settled out of court.

Presumably the photographer involved did not obtain permission from the owner of the launch for its use as a prop in glamour photography, and this is a point all photographers should remember. There are some beautiful old houses and similar settings which make superb locations for photography, glamour or otherwise. There is no harm in using them providing the owner and the occupier (if not one and the same) consent not only to the use of the location but for the type of photography the location is being used for. Without that consent the photographer is not only trespassing but possibly laying himself open to an action for libel.

In 1957 a magazine published an article which painted Canvey Island in Essex as an island of sin. The whole piece was hyperbolic and may well have been written tongue in cheek. The only problem was that in illustrating the article the magazine published a photograph of The Canvey Island Club with a caption which read: "Social Centre – The Canvey Island Club is open in the evenings."

The owner sued, claiming that the article and photograph meant she ran a disreputable club where immorality, swearing and gaming took place. She was awarded £100 damages.

In *Watson v IPC Transport Press Ltd (1982)*, the plaintiff claimed that a magazine published a photograph of him, mending the outboard motor of his yacht on a marina quayside in France, to illustrate an article about a mysterious thief who was stealing pontoons from the marina. It was run under the heading "Marina Thief". The magazine claimed the article was a joke, which must have impressed the jury since they awarded only one halfpenny in damages.

Problems with captions

It is not reported what damages were paid by a national newspaper which, in reporting a girl's elopement to Scotland, mistakenly published the photograph of another girl of the same name. The case was settled by way of an apology and the making of a statement in open court, plus an agreed sum by way of damages.

This case shows the danger of using stock photographs without checking on whether the person depicted is the right one, or whether the photograph depicts a person who, in the circumstances, is relevant to the report it is accompanying.

Among past cases was an action brought by a Smithfield meat porter against a national newspaper which used a stock photograph of him to illustrate an article on pilfering from the market. The innuendo was clear: the porter was guilty of stealing meat. He received a sum of money in damages.

So did a model whose photograph was taken from stock and used to promote a product as being good for expectant mothers. Until the advertising agency which created the advertisement heard from the model's solicitors, little did they know that not only was she not an expectant mother, she was not married either.

Earlier in this chapter mention has been made of how a comparatively innocent and thoroughly innocuous statement can, because of innuendo, lead to a libel action. a good example this, from the point of view of a newspaper, is Cassidy's case. There is a positive duty on the part of the photographer to ensure with as much certainty as he can that a caption which accompanies a photograph is accurate and unlikely to cause legal problems.

It is very common in the provincial press, trade publications and some magazines for group photographs to be taken at social occasions depicting people with glasses in their hand. It is also quite common, although dangerous, for a caption to refer to a group "enjoying a drink" at such and such an occasion.

On the surface there is no harm in that, but one of that group may be known as a teetotaller with strong views on drink. The liquid in the glass that particular person is holding may be a tonic or a mineral water, but if the caption implies that they are drinking alcohol the teetotaller may be in a very good position to bring an action for libel.

It would not be difficult for that person to prove he or she had been held in contempt or ridiculed on the grounds of hypocritical behaviour, of holding himself or herself out as a teetotaller and then be described as "enjoying a drink" with all that that connotes to the average man in the street.

In most, if not all, cases of libel in which photographs are involved, it is, as has been demonstrated above, the innuendo which has caused trouble, and this is almost always generated by a caption. But one can conceive of cases where it is the absence of a caption that causes problems.

There are a number of well known campaigners against pornography, some of whom have carried out genuine research in Soho, and photographs of them doing so have appeared in the media from time to time with an explanatory caption or accompanying story.

But if one of those persons was pictured entering a cinema renowned for showing soft porn films and the picture published or exhibited without any caption, the innuendo would be clear: that person was a hypocrite, for the assumption would be that he was visiting such an establishment for pleasure. Yet another example of the care which must be taken in publishing photographs in such circumstances.

Doctoring and manipulation

A great source of danger is the doctored photograph: a picture altered either by use of an airbrush to paint out part of it, the creation of a montage, or other means of altering the visual picture depicted.

That was how previous editions of this book started this particular section. But the dangers inherent in the alterations outlined above have greatly increased due to rapid advances in technology. Digital manipulation or enhancement of photographs is now such that a person in a photograph can literally be depicted standing on his head.

To illustrate the dangers inherent in doctoring, manipulation, enhancement or call it what you will, there is an old Fleet Street story going back many years, which may or may not be apocryphal.

A Press Lord was showing his wife the layout and pictures for the following day's paper, a paper which, incidentally, had a great appeal to "genteel" ladies. One of the pictures to be published was that of a prize bull at a Smithfield livestock exhibition. It wasn't the bull that horrified the wife, but that part of his anatomy which would make the bull in demand for breeding. This, she insisted, was something that would alarm and offend the susceptibilities of "genteel" readers, so her husband ordered the offending organ to be painted out.

The result, the story goes, was that a threat of legal action rapidly followed, with the owner of the bull complaining that he had been made to look ridiculous by the emasculation of his prize animal.

The story may not be true, but it is an amusing and instructive example of the dangers which can follow when a picture is altered by whatever means.

Recently *The Observer* newspaper published an article with a headline amending the old saying "lies, damn lies and statistics" to "lies, damn lies and photojournalism". Unfortunately this seems to be becoming more and more a truism.

One of the most common forms of doctoring is to manipulate photographs of well known politicians or other celebrities, placing their heads onto another person's body or putting them into a different context to produce a satirical effect.

A recent instance which was widely reported concerned John Prescott, the deputy leader of the Labour Party. The London *Evening Standard* published a photograph of Mr Prescott at a social function supposingly sipping champagne with his wife, under the heading "Champagne socialist". In the original photograph Mr Prescott had a bottle of beer beside him, but by use of a computer the beer bottle disappeared from the photograph while a crop transformed Mrs Prescott's bottle to one that suggested it contained champagne.

It is arguable that the alteration of the photograph together with the heading could have suggested that Mr Prescott was leading a social life at variance with his political beliefs. This might well have been held to be libellous if he had chosen to initiate proceedings for defamation. Having dismissing the original complaint as a "storm in a beer bottle", the editor subsequently realised that such a picture devalued all photographs in the paper, and he apologised.

Another instance cited by *The Observer* was a complaint against cable channel Live TV by the Royal family. The company had published an advertisement in which a doctored photograph depicted Princess Diana being kissed by footballer Paul Gascoigne at her wedding, rather than by Prince Charles her husband. The complaint was upheld by the Advertising Standards Authority.

One of the reasons why image manipulation is rife may be due to ignorance of the law; but more likely publishers take a chance that, since it is only those regularly in the public eye who are "victims" of manipulation, they will view such publication with an amused tolerance.

That is not to say that the inherent danger of someone, whether in the public eye or not, bringing an action for defamation will go away. With the onus of establishing that an offending publication was not defamatory resting with the publisher, who is to say that a judge may not rule that such a manipulated image is capable of bearing a defamatory meaning, with a jury agreeing that it was defamatory?

It is a sobering thought that back in 1980 the actress Brigitte Bardot sued the publishers of a French magazine for publishing a faked, and unflattering, photograph of her. The court held that the impression of age given, even though that impression was exaggerated and almost a caricature, *did* damage the reputation of Mlle Bardot. She was awarded FF22,500 in damages.

Who is to say that a similar situation could not happen in this country?

Criminal libel

Unlike libel in a civil action, where publication to a third party has to be proved (although in the case of newspapers it is presumed), in a prosecution for criminal libel it is only necessary to prove publication to the person libelled. Furthermore, a person accused of criminal libel has to prove not only the truth of the libel, but that publication was for the public benefit.

The reason for this onerous duty placed on a defendant to prove that publication was for the public benefit, and the reason why there is such an offence of criminal libel – a criminal rather than a civil wrong – is because publication might lead to a breach of the peace or seriously affect the reputation of the person libelled.

One of the most famous cases of criminal libel in recent years was that brought by Sir James Goldsmith against the magazine *Private Eye*. Sir James told magistrates hearing the committal proceedings: "When a campaign of vilification takes place the repercussions can sometimes lead to a breach of the peace."

However, under Section 8 of the *Law of Libel (Amendment) Act 1888*, it is necessary for a High Court judge to give permission for a prosecution for a case of criminal libel against a publisher. It appears that in this case the judge who granted permission for the prosecution to take place accepted that it was not an essential ingredient of the offence to prove the likelihood of a breach of the peace occurring.

In the event the case did not come to trial, as the parties came to terms and Sir James withdrew his private prosecution.

If the person who published the criminal libel knew it to be false he may be fined or imprisoned for up to two years, but if he was unaware of the falsity, the maximum term of imprisonment is one year.

In past cases involving criminal libel it has always been the publication of words which has led to a prosecution. In a Court of Criminal Appeal judgment in *R v Wicks (1936)* the point was made as follows: "...words written of a man which are likely to provoke him to commit a breach of the peace or, if seen by others, to hold him up to hatred, ridicule or contempt or damage his reputation."

But it does not take much imagination to see how a candid camera shot linked with a caption, or a digitally manipulated picture, could do just that.

There is one other point upon which a prosecution for criminal libel can be based and that is when the libel seriously affects the reputation of the person defamed. However criminal prosecutions for this type of libel are extremely rare, and as has been noted earlier they can only be initiated with the consent of a High Court judge.

Among other categories of libel which could affect a photographer is that of obscene libel. But this is rarely, if ever, heard of today because, in the case of photographs, any action would be more likely to be a criminal prosecution under the *Obscene Publications Acts*, dealt with in a later chapter.

Defences to libel

If it can be proved that the plaintiff agreed to publication, that is a complete defence. This underlines the value of getting permission from those who figure in photographs.

It will be remembered that one of the dangers which could face a photographer is that of innuendo. The example of a prominent anti-pornography campaigner entering a Soho sex shop or strip club has been cited. Similarly, while the fact that a person enters a public house is not by itself pejorative, if the same person was pictured staggering out of licensed premises, to many people there would be a clear innuendo that the person was, to say the least, the worse for drink. But he might not be; he could be feeling faint, or have tripped over a piece of torn floor covering, or encountered some other mishap which caused him to stagger. Hence the importance of obtaining consent to publish the photograph.

If known, the purpose of publication should be included in a release, and even, if at all possible, the caption to be used agreed and included in the form.

Another defence is that the libel has already been adjudged. All this really means is that the case has already been either heard and disposed of by a court, or by a settlement announced in court. But it must be remembered that the fact that one publication has already been dealt with does not mean that another publication can claim that the matter has been settled, as every further publication of a defamatory statement is a fresh cause of action.

To return to the example of the teetotaller said to be enjoying a drink. That person could have brought a libel action which could have been settled out of court, and as far as the first publication of photograph and offending caption is concerned the matter has ended.

Or rather there the matter should have ended, because a competent picture librarian would have removed the offending caption and fixed a note to the photograph explaining the libel which was contained in the caption. Normally this would be sufficient, but life has a perverse habit of distributing banana skins for the unwary. If by any chance there was cause to use the picture again, and the warning note of the conscientious librarian had been detached, the photograph could appear with a similar offending caption. This would be a fresh publication and a fresh cause for an action for libel.

As an interesting footnote, in 1981 a regional newspaper re-published, in a "Looking Back" column, a statement made about a doctor 25 years previously. The statement was libellous, but had gone unnoticed by the doctor at the time of first publication. However, on seeing it repeated he took action and received damages.

This only emphasises the care that needs to be taken with

library pictures. It is better to destroy a contentious photograph than run the risk of inadvertently publishing it in the future and thereby attracting a further action for defamation.

Justification

Justification, with one exception, is a complete defence to a libel action, though as far as photographs are concerned it could never apply to those that have been doctored.

To prove justification it is necessary to show the words complained of are true in substance and in fact. Substitute "photograph" for "words" and it can be seen clearly how a defence of justification must fail with a doctored photograph.

However, a libel is most likely to be committed in a caption. This demonstrates how great care must be taken when writing a caption, a comment or any other wording to accompany a photograph for either publication in print, an exhibition, or electronic transmission.

One further point, which is so important that it cannot be stressed strongly enough, is that not only must the words complained of be justified, so too must any innuendo.

The exception to the rule that truth is a complete defence against an action for libel is to be found in the *Rehabilitation of Offenders Act 1974*. This act laid down that a convicted criminal who has served a sentence of no more than thirty months imprisonment will, after a period of ten years, be considered as rehabilitated. The actual amount of time which must pass before a person can claim to be rehabilitated as far as conviction is concerned, and can claim that the conviction is spent depends, surprisingly enough, not on the severity of the crime but on the sentence imposed.

If a spent conviction is revealed and the defence of justification raised, the defence can be negated if malice on the part of the publisher can be proved. This demonstrates yet again the care which must be taken with the writing of captions.

Fair comment

Another defence which is much used in that of fair comment.

It is now more than likely that a manipulated photograph could be the subject of a defamation action, for which a possible defence would be that of fair comment. Fair comment might also be used as a defence if a plaintiff sued on the grounds that a caption to a photograph was defamatory.

To succeed in a defence of fair comment it is necessary to show that the matter complained of was the honestly held opinion of the writer, that it was made in good faith and without malice on a matter of public interest, and that the facts upon which the comment was made were true.

It is not necessary to convince a jury that the comment expressed views which would be held by a reasonable man; indeed, the views may well be unreasonable, but if they are the honestly held opinion of the writer and the comment does not impute base or dishonourable motives, the defence will succeed.

Privilege

The defence of privilege for fair and accurate reports of judicial proceedings in the United Kingdom was created in the *Law of Libel (Amendment) Act 1888* and was always referred to as "absolute privilege" even though this was not the phrase used in the legislation. The *Defamation Act 1996*, however, incorporated the phrase "absolute privilege" into legislation and extended the defence to cover not only judicial proceedings in the United Kingdom, but also reports of proceedings of the European Court of Justice, the European Court of Human Rights and international war crime tribunals, and defined a court as any tribunal or body exercising the judicial power of the state.

The 1996 Act also amended the 1952 Act by giving, *inter alia*, qualified privilege to fair and accurate reports of proceedings in public of a legislature, court or a public inquiry anywhere in the world.

There are a number of other areas where privilege may be invoked. These are unlikely to affect any but press and media photographers, or reporters who may also be acting as photographers in the new era of "multi-skilling". Nevertheless, in that context they are significant enough to detail here.

The qualified privilege the 1952 Act gave to statements for which the defence of qualified privilege can be raised *without* the need of a publication publishing a letter by way of explanation or contradiction continues; so does the defence of qualified privilege where it is necessary to publish a letter or statement by way of explanation or contradiction.

Qualified privilege without the need of publishing the type of statement referred to in the previous paragraph, applies to fair and accurate reports of proceedings in public of a legislature anywhere in the world, or a government appointed inquiry anywhere in the world. Protection is also granted to an extract or a fair and accurate copy of any document or register which, by law, is open to inspection by the public. Similar protection is given to a notice published by a court, a judge or officer of a court anywhere in the world.

Qualified privilege with the need to publish a statement will cover a fair and accurate copy or extract of a notice issued to the public for or on behalf of any member state of the European Union, European Parliament any international organisation, or of a document made available by either the European Court of Justice, a court of a European Union state or by a judge or officer of any such court.

It also extends protection to (in this country): a meeting of a local authority; a public meeting; a meeting of magistrates not acting as a court as would be the case when they sit as licensing justices; a tribunal, commission, committee or a statement made by someone appointed for any inquiry by either the Crown, a minister of government, or a local authority.

Similar protection is continued for reports of findings and/or decisions of bodies which are empowered to control art, science, sport, learning, business, trade or industry, a charity or a profession and religion. This includes statements issued by The Law Society, the Bar Council, the General Medical Council, the Jockey Club, the Football Association and many more bodies.

Qualified privilege also covers statements by the government or any authority which performs functions of government, including the police and local authorities. Curiously this privilege does not extend to notices issued by NHS Trusts, although there is provision in the Act for these bodies to be included by way of a statutory instrument being laid before Parliament.

Like the defence of fair comment, the defence of qualified privilege can be undermined by malice on the part of the writer and/or publisher.

Other options and time limits

The *Defamation Act 1996* also laid down a fast-track procedure for dealing with certain libel actions, by giving a judge the power to dispose of such an action summarily by awarding damages of no more than £10,000 and ordering publication of a suitable correction or apology. A judge is also empowered to dismiss a claim which he considers has no possibility of success.

The Act also introduced a new "offer of amends" defence by which a publication which has innocently defamed a person can offer an apology, a payment of damages and any legal costs.

The time limit for bringing an action for libel is one year from the date of publication, but a court has the power to extend this. Such would be the case if a person was defamed while he was out of the country and the libel was not brought to his attention until he returned after the time limit had expired. However, it is expected that the power to extend the time limit will only be used after a rigorous examination of all the factors involved.

Because the majority of libel actions are what are known as personal, they die with the death of the plaintiff. The reason for this being the case, rather than letting an action continue for the benefit of the plaintiff's estate, is that not being alive the plaintiff is unable to care about his reputation.

Some final points

In recent years juries have awarded damages which have been, to say the least, astronomical, bearing no relation to the injury the libel may have caused.

Fortunately for publishers, in 1990 the Court of Appeal was given the right to vary the amount of damages awarded by a jury. Judges and counsel can also now point out to juries the sums awarded by way of damages in personal injury actions, and draw a comparison with the libel in question. Judges can also provide guidance to a jury which might be considering an award of exemplary damages.

It is necessary to sound a warning about the publication of corrections: great care must be taken when phrasing an apology and/or correction so as to make certain that a fresh libel has not been committed. It is in circumstances such as these that it is desirable to take expert advice.

Because legal aid is not available for actions for defamation, some litigants have brought cases under the heading of malicious falsehood, for which legal aid is available. Briefly, a malicious falsehood imputes no blamewordy action towards the plaintiff, but is actionable because it could cause the plaintiff financial loss.

Using a photograph of the wrong person could lead to a claim for malicious damage. For example, if a well known solicitor or doctor is to retire, and in carrying the story a newspaper published a photograph of the wrong person. If this caused his clients and/or patients – or indeed, if a businessman, his customers – to cease to use his services, a case for damages for malicious falsehood could be established.

However, because damage has to be proved it is necessary for the plaintiff to show financial loss.

One final word of explanation: the use of the word malicious does not mean that the newspaper which published the wrong photograph did so out of spite or ill-will towards the wronged person. Malice is used here in the sense of recklessness, in not caring or finding out whether or not the photograph published was truly that of the person concerned.

This serves to underline the importance of ensuring that picture files are kept as accurately and as up to date as possible.

5   Obscenity

"Dirty pictures; feelthy postcards" are older than the camera itself. The terms conjure up pedlars in Oriental bazaars, or the touts and seedy back street bookshops of Soho and other major cities throughout the world.

In recent years the frontiers of what can be published have been expanded with breathtaking speed; prior to and during the Second World War, quality magazines like *Lilliput* and *Men Only* had discreetly posed photographs of nude female models which revealed little but left a lot to the imagination. Today all that has changed; everything is revealed and nothing left to the imagination. Photographs in certain magazines and in some raunchier newspapers depict couples or groups in simulated sex and almost anything goes.

To most people obscenity is equated with sexual acts or perversions, but it must be remembered it also includes extreme violence. Obscenity is also subjective; what is considered to be obscene to one person may not be to another.

The law relating to obscenity is to be found in the *Obscene Publications Acts 1959* and *1964*. The 1959 Act codified and put into statute form what used to be known as obscene libels, although the old common law offence remains. Photographs have very often been the subject of prosecution under these Acts.

Tests and definitions

From time to time magazines are seized by the police and either made the subject of a destruction order or, on rare occasions, a prosecution.

The test of obscenity is whether the offending material would tend to corrupt or deprave those likely to be corrupted. This test can be applied to a series of photographs so that if one is deemed to be obscene, technically, the others would be similar condemned. Indeed in *R v Anderson (1972)* it was held that if a magazine consisted, as it normally does, of a series of articles, each had to be considered separately, but if one was deemed to be obscene, the whole publication would be contaminated by that obscenity.

Because most cases of obscenity are considered in the light of the social and moral conditions obtaining at the time, the boundaries of obscenity vary enormously. It is also conceivable that a jury drawn from those living in a quiet and comparatively isolated country district might well take a different view on obscenity to that of twelve men and women from a sophisticated inner city area.

It is no defence for an accused to claim that offending material could not corrupt its reading or viewing public because it was intended for those who were already corrupt; the crux of offences under the Acts is publication of offending material. "Publication" in this context means distributing, lending, circulating, selling, giving, hiring or offering for sale or hire, obscene material.

Under the *Broadcasting Act 1990* the 1959 Act was extended to cover television and sound broadcasting as well as books and films. There can be no prosecution without the consent of the Director of Public Prosecutions, but a magistrate, if satisfied that reasonable grounds exist to believe an offence has been committed, may authorise the police to require that any sound and/or visual recording of the broadcast be handed over.

In the case of *R v Arnold (1996)* the Court of Appeal held that images made available to others via the Internet constituted an "act of publication", in this case liable under the *Obscene Publications Act*.

No offence is committed by a person who buys or reads or views obscene material. However, even the giving or lending of obscene material is enough to constitute publication, although nearly all prosecutions have involved material offered for sale. But a cautionary note must be sounded at this juncture: the *Protection of Children Act 1978* makes it an offence to possess an indecent photograph of a child without a legitimate reason – this is looked at in greater detail later.

Prosecution and defence

Prosecutions under the Acts usually take one of two forms. The first is seizure of offending material, after either the police or the Director of Public Prosecutions have been granted a warrant by a magistrate. The onus is then on the publisher or retailer to prove to magistrates that the material is not obscene and should not be forfeited or destroyed. There is no right of trial by jury if this course of action is brought and in most cases forfeiture orders are made by magistrates.

Section 2(5) of the 1959 Act provides a defence if the accused can prove he had not examined the article in question and had no reason to know it was obscene. This defence is one that could hardly be successfully argued by a photographer who took photographs alleged to be obscene.

The defence of what can best be described as publication for the public good has been used on several occasions. The 1959 Act introduced this defence if publication was: "..in the interests of science, literature, art or learning or other objects of public concern."

To establish this defence successfully, the defence has to produce witnesses to state that in their opinion publication is justified on the grounds that it is in the interest of art, literature, science or learning. The defence was first used in 1960 when Penguin Books was prosecuted for publishing *Lady Chatterley's Lover*.

Since then it has been used on several occasions and has resulted in the delightful, if unedifying, spectacle of expert witnesses from various fields being called by the prosecution to rebut the defence's own experts!

Photographs of children

Closely allied to obscenity is the regrettable use of children in pornographic photographs. Until quite recently there was a gap in the law: although a photograph involving a child was obscene, there was no indecency on the part of the photographer as far as the child or children was concerned provided that the photographer did not commit an act of indecency on them.

To fill this gap the *Protection of Children Act* was passed in 1978. This makes it an offence to take any indecent photograph of a child as well as to distribute or show such photographs, or even to possess them with the object of distributing or showing them to others.

There is a defence under this Act of having a legitimate reason for exhibiting, possessing or distributing such photographs. Here the accused must show he had not seen them himself or did not know, or expect them to be, indecent. Again this is an impossible defence for the photographer who actually took the photographs to raise and sustain.

Note that the offence can also be committed by a body managed by its members, such as a photographic club.

Although the Act prohibits the taking of indecent photographs of a child, there is no definition of what constitutes indecency. In any prosecution under the Act magistrates or jurors would be expected to take an objective view, although, because of the natural revulsion such photographs raise in any right-thinking person, it would be impossible for subjective views not to impinge on what should be a clinically judicial decision.

In any event, prosecutions can only be brought with the consent of the Director of Public Prosecutions or the Crown Prosecution Service. It is most likely that in arriving at a decision, the authorities would ask: "Would magistrates or a jury, if properly directed by either their clerk or a judge, be likely to find the photograph indecent?"

In all probability there would be a further question to answer: "Is there a 51 per cent chance or more of the case resulting in a conviction?"

There have not been a great many cases brought under the Act and it is likely, by the nature of pornographic pictures, that most, if not all, of these cases referred to possession of pictures rather than the actual taking of them, and probably formed part of a series of charges involving a paedophile ring.

In the summer of 1996 an American from Southern California was convicted by magistrates at Bournemouth of taking indecent pictures of young children. He had been seen by beach inspectors employed by the local authority, videoing "nothing in particular" for "hours on end". When police investigated the man and his equipment, it was found that his camcorder had been fitted with a mirror and a false lens to enable it to record naked children playing on one side of the beach. At the time it was reported that there had been ten similar cases in Bournemouth alone, which were then working their way through the courts.

In 1995 a well known television newsreader had the misfortune to receive nationwide publicity because a photo processor passed what he thought were indecent photographs – of her daughter in the bath – to the police. Of course there was no indecency, and it is regrettable that the news reader was the victim of such unwelcome and unwarranted publicity.

There have, however, been a number of less publicised but very similar cases involving ordinary members of the public being reported to the police by high street processors. In some cases quite innocent family snapshots have given rise to arrests and prosecutions, simply because a naked child appeared in a photograph. These cases highlight the risks that anyone can run when taking photographs of children.

Partly as a result of the well-publicised case mentioned above, in mid-1996 the Photo Marketing Association, the major trade body for the consumer processing industry, put together a set of guidelines for processors to refer to. These guidelines are dealt with fully at the end of this chapter.

Postal regulations

Allied with obscenity as far as photographs are concerned is the question of sending indecent or obscene material through the post – an offence under Section 11 of the *Post Office Act 1953*.

What is of particular interest in a potential prosecution under this Act is that the test of what is or is not obscene is different to that in the *Obscene Publications Acts*. Here the test refers to matter which is "grossly offensive or of an indecent or obscene character." To obtain convictions under the *Obscene Publications Acts* it is necessary to show that the material has a tendency to "corrupt or deprave", which is a much higher standard than "grossly offensive or of an indecent or obscene character."

This point was underlined in *R v Anderson (1974)*, in which a publication called *Oz* was convicted of offences under both the *Obscene Publications Acts* and the *Post Office Act*. On appeal, the conviction of the editor under the former act was quashed, but convictions under the *Post Office Act* were upheld.

Although the lack of a definition of what is obscene, indecent or grossly offensive may seem tiresome, it must be remembered that it is almost impossible to create a definition to fit all circumstances and conditions. Furthermore, the advantage of what some might think to be too widely drawn an offence is that it enables the social mores of the time to be taken into account before a prosecution is launched.

Other offences

There are a number of other offences concerning obscenity, many of which are rarely used today. One is the *Vagrancy Acts 1824* and *1898*, which created the offence of exposing to view in a public place an obscene or indecent picture.

It must be remembered that obscene or indecent photographs may also be subject to local bye-laws. However, prosecution under any bye-law is likely to be rare, as any indecent or obscene photograph is more likely to be prosecuted under one or other of the Acts discussed earlier.

The PMA processing guidelines

As mentioned earlier, the Birmingham based Photo Marketing Association now issues guidelines for processors, and the author is greatly indebted to the PMA for its permission to paraphrase them here. Before doing so, however, it is worth noting that the guidelines have been considered by the association's solicitors and the opinion of Queen's Counsel has also been obtained.

The purpose of the guidelines is to help photo processors and retailers to be aware of their legal position with regard to processing and printing of indecent and obscene photographs and other dubious material – and what to do if offered such matter by a customer.

Quite rightly the document states that processors have to observe the law of the land and cannot reasonably be expected by customers to process and return material which could well mean that processors were themselves committing a criminal offence. The introduction to the guidelines also states that "there is a particular responsibility in relation to indecent photographs of children as the circumstances may indicate that the child is in need of care and protection."

The unspoken thought behind this statement, obviously, is that the child may be the victim of sexual abuse.

Processors are reminded that they should handle "the very rare cases" when potentially indecent or obscene photographs are received with sensitivity and discretion. But if they feel the photographs give serious cause for concern, they will need to consult the relevant authorities so that they(the authorities) may decide whether the material warrants further investigation and/or prosecution.

After noting that only the courts can decide what is indecent or obscene, the guidelines set out guidance which has been collated from police and other sources.

PHOTOGRAPHS OF CHILDREN:

Stressing that each photograph should be judged individually and noting, as has been noted earlier in this chapter, that there is no statutory definition of what is or is not indecent, points which suggest that a photograph of a child could be indecent potentially, include:

1. Does the child appear to be under 16 years of age?;
2. Is the child aware the photograph is being taken (posed)?;
3. Are the genitalia exposed?;
4. Does the photograph have a gratuitously sexual implication?;
5. Is it indecent by virtue of the context?

As far as the latter is concerned, the guidelines suggest that if a child is included in the same photograph as sexually active adults this could be – and probably is in the view of the author of this book – indecent.

The guidelines point out that if processor knowingly processed or printed indecent material involving children they may be committing a criminal offence if the material was returned to the customer.

The recommendation is that a processor who receives material he believes to be potentially indecent should contact the police for further advice, and in the case of photographs involving children, the local Child Protection Unit.

PHOTOGRAPHS OF ADULTS:

Nudity or posing in itself will not render a photograph obscene say the guidelines, which then go on to outline activities which, if depicted in a photograph, are likely to do so. They are:

1. Sexual penetration;

2. Masturbation;
3. Sado-masochism/bondage;
4. Unnatural sexual practices or perversions.

After stressing that processors may commit a criminal offence under the *Obscene Publication Acts* if such material is processed and returned and then subsequently published, the advice is not to return either the prints or negatives unless they are satisfied that the material is not obscene and will not be published. Processors are also asked to consider seeking advice from their local CID.

HANDLING CASES:

It is recommended that processors develop internal procedures for dealing with rare cases of potentially obscene material, and introduce a system so that an employee who has doubts about a photograph refers it immediately to a director or manager. Where possible it is also suggested that a committee of three should rule on the photograph, giving reasons in writing contemporaneously for the decision they have reached.

Processors are warned not to return either the negatives or the prints to the customer but instead give them to the police if they are requested to do so.

Furthermore processors are warned not to accuse the customer of taking or having indecent or obscene photographs as this is a matter for a court to decide. All the processor should do is to inform the customer that due to the nature of the photographs they have been referred to the police for their advice. Stress is also laid on the need for all people involved – staff, suppliers, police, etc – to be aware of the need for the incident to be kept confidential.

Not only should processors keep detailed notes of the incident for use should they be called as a witness in a subsequent prosecution, they are also reminded to ensure that any communication with customers on these issues are handled with discretion and sensitivity. It is also pointed out that if the matter is discussed with a customer it should be in private where the conversation cannot be overheard.

Processors are reminded that the law will look for reasonableness, and that a decision by a processor to refer or not to refer suspect photographs to the police is soundly based and founded on proper grounds, not on the whim or the idiosyncrasies of some unbalanced individual. Reasonableness, it is said, would also be a defence not only to a civil action but of the offence of publishing under the *Obscene Publications Acts*.

The PMA guidelines recognise that other material may be submitted for processing which does not fall into the categories outlined above.

The guidelines observe that many processors would not expect their staff to handle material which might not be illegal *per se*, but are morally or otherwise offensive. Included in this are photographs depicting the commission of a crime, such as dog or badger baiting, the use of illegal substances such as cocaine, or glue sniffing.

Processors have the right to refuse to handle material if they do not wish to do so. It is pointed out that if this is the case – and while it may be inappropriate to involve the police – the processor should quietly discuss with the customer why the order has not been carried out, should return the negatives but destroy any prints, and request that no further similar material be submitted in the future. No charge should be made.

Finally, because of the *Post Office Act*, processors are advised that when they are able to return indecent material to customers it should not be sent by post but made available for collection or sent by courier.

These eminently sensible guidelines should be followed not only by processors but by all involved in photography.

6 State Security

One of the oddities of law in this country is that, not having a written constitution, there is no legislation which clearly states what a citizen can lawfully do. The rights of a citizen are often outlined and contained in legislation as will be seen in later chapters in this book, but there is very little in law which states what a citizen can do; rather our law – especially the criminal law – states what may *not* be done.

As far as this and the following two chapters are concerned, we will concentrate on when it may be an offence to take photographs. It is worth remembering that here we are dealing with the criminal law, which contains provisions for fines and/or imprisonment as the ultimate sanction a court can impose to mark society's displeasure towards those who break the law – even though such transgression may have been innocent and in ignorance of the law.

The question of intention

One of the main elements of criminal law, indeed the touchstone which runs through most legislation which contains penal sanctions, is contained in the Latin expression *actus non facit reum nisi mens sit rea*. This means that an act does not of itself constitute guilt unless there is a guilty mind or intention. More simply this can be explained as an intention to commit a criminal offence. Thus, to give a simple example, a person can take a sum of money from a shop till but commits no offence unless its removal is accompanied by an intention not to return it, thus depriving the owner permanently of his money.

But there is also what is known to the law as an "absolute" offence, in which it is not necessary to prove a guilty mind or an intention to commit the offence – the mere commission of the offence is sufficient to convict the person concerned. This type of offence is most usually found in road traffic cases or in legislation passed to enforce standards in public conduct.

Also there are a number of words used in legislation which courts over the years have construed as meaning that *mens rea* is required before a person can be found guilty. Words like "knowingly", "wilfully", "maliciously", "permitting" or "suffering", used in legislation which has a penal element, denote the need to prove an accused person had a guilty intention before they can be convicted of an offence.

With this explanation in mind, it is now possible to look at those criminal offences a photographer can be guilty of during the course of his employment or simply in following his hobby.

The Official Secrets Act

A photographer is particularly at risk when taking photographs of military equipment or installations, and may thereby be in breach of the *Official Secrets Acts 1911, 1920* and *1939*, which the courts construe as one Act. Unfortunately the Acts have been drafted – either intentionally or by accident – in such a way that a person who has no intention of passing information of a confidential or secret nature can be ensnared, and photographers are very much at risk.

It is necessary to look at the Acts in detail. Section 1 of the 1911 Act makes it an offence punishable by up to 14 years imprisonment if a person for any purpose prejudicial to the safety or interest of the state:

1. Approaches, inspects, passes over or is in the neighbourhood or enters any prohibited place;
2. Makes any sketch, plan, model or note which might be, or is intended to be, useful to an enemy;
3. Obtains, collects, records or communicates to any person information that might be, or is intended to be, useful to an enemy.

As can be seen this is very wide ranging and would include photographs. What then is a prohibited place within the meaning of the Act? The answer is to be found in Section 3 of the 1911 Act, as amended by the 1920 Act:

(a) any work of defence, arsenal, naval or air force establishment or station, factory, dockyard, mine, minefield, camp, ship or aircraft belonging to or occupied by or on behalf of Her Majesty, or any telegraph, telephone, wireless or signal station, or office so belonging or occupied and any place occupied by and on behalf of Her Majesty and used for the purpose of building, repairing, making or storing any munitions of war, or any sketches, note or model relating thereto, or for the purpose of getting any metals, oil or mineral of use in time of war;

(b) any place not belonging to Her Majesty where any munitions of war, or any sketches, etc., related thereto, are made, repaired, gotten or stored under contract with, or with any person on behalf of, Her Majesty;

(c) any place belonging to or used for the purpose of Her Majesty which is for the time being declared by order of a Secretary of State to be a prohibited place for the purpose of this section on the ground that information in respect thereto, or damage thereto, would be useful to an enemy;

(d) any railway, road, way or channel, or other means of communication by land or water (including any works or structure for gas, water, electricity or other works of a public character) or any place where munitions of war, or any sketches etc. relating thereto are being made, repaired or stored otherwise than on behalf of Her Majesty, which for the time being declared by order of a Secretary of State to be a prohibited place for the purpose of this section, on the ground that information with respect thereto, or the destruction or obstruction thereof, would be useful to an enemy.

Interpretation of the Acts

The above section repays careful study for, in effect, is is capable of bringing within the criminal law any photographer who innocently takes a photograph of any of these many and varied places. However, prosecutions under the Acts can only be brought with the consent of the Attorney-General, and it is fortunate that usually a robust and commonsense view is taken these days.

To take an example, photographs have often appeared of the top secret Government Communications Headquarters in Cheltenham which, strictly speaking, is an offence under the Acts. But obviously the fact that this particular building is well known to be what in fact it is, means that photographing the exterior is likely to do little harm to state security.

Most buildings which are covered by the Acts display a notice to this effect. Photographers are more likely to be at risk under the Acts if they take photographs of more dramatic pieces of military equipment such as aeroplanes, tanks, guns, vessels, etc., which are regarded by the authorities as top secret but which carry no notices saying they are covered by the Acts. Some may even be the subject of a DA Notice, a topic dealt with later in this chapter.

Throughout Section 1 of the Act runs the thread that obtaining or receiving information must be for a purpose prejudicial to the State, but nowhere is there a definition of what is meant by the term "prejudicial". Indeed, it seems that prejudicial can be anything that a Secretary of State or an Attorney-General of the day considers it to be.

This was exemplified in 1962 when six members of what was then known as the Committee of 100, strongly opposed to nuclear weapons, staged a sit-in at an East Anglian airfield and were arrested and charged under Section 1 of the Act. There was clearly no question of espionage involved, but the then Attorney General felt the demonstration, peaceful though it was, amounted to sabotage. The six were convicted and on appeal, which was finally heard by the House of Lords, the conviction was upheld.

So it presents little difficulty for an Attorney-General of the day who is so minded to order a prosecution against a photographer who, although in no way connected with any espionage agency, might enter a prohibited place inadvertently or photograph a piece of top secret military equipment without realising it. The photographer would have to rely on the common sense of a jury to recognise that no *mens rea* was involved and acquit him.

Section 2 and the Official Secrets Act 1989

Perhaps the most criticised of all penal legislation has been Section 2 of the Act. Known as the "catch-all" section, its scope has been rightly criticised by members of the judiciary, the legal profession, journalists and civil libertarians, to say nothing of members of both Houses of Parliament.

It became known as the "catch-all" section because it made it an offence for a person to reveal or publish a wide range of information which had no bearing whatsoever on the security of the realm.

In 1989 a new Official Secrets Act was passed which, although described as a "liberalising measure", encountered strong opposition from both sides of the House of Commons as well as from journalists and those with an interest in civil liberties.

Section 5 of the 1989 Act made it an offence for a member of the public – which of course includes a photographer or journalist – to disclose information without lawful authority if they knew or had reasonable cause to believe that it was protected against disclosure. Such information must have been received without lawful authority from a Crown servant or government contractor, or received in confidence. Again, the person who received the information must know or have reasonable cause to believe the information was received in these circumstances, so the *mens rea* element is retained in the new Act.

As far as the "in confidence" is concerned, the prosecution has to prove that a journalist (and this could easily include a photographer who was allowed to photograph a document) had been told the information was given in confidence, or the circumstances were such that the person making the information available could reasonably suppose that the information was being imparted under the cloak of confidence.

The six classes of information are:

1. Security and intelligence;
2. Defence;
3. International relations;
4. Crime;
5. Information on government telephone tapping, interception of letters or other communications;
6. Information entrusted in confidence to other states or international organisations.

There are a number of defences available for those who publish what is termed "protected information" one of which is that no harm was done by the publication of that information.

Protection of sources

There is one other section of the 1920 Act which can be applied in a particularly restrictive and, some would claim, oppressive manner to photographers. This especially affects those in the media who may have been supplied with photographs or negatives which are the subject of prohibition under the Act. Section 6 reads:

"(1) Where a chief officer of police is satisfied that there is a reasonable ground for suspecting that an offence under Section 1 (of the 1911 Act) has been committed and for believing that any person is able to furnish information as to the offence, he may apply to the Secretary of State for permission to exercise the powers conferred by the Secretary of State and, if such permission is granted, he may authorise a superintendent of police, or any police officer not below the rank of inspector, to require the person believed to be able to furnish information to give any information in his power relating to the offence or suspected offence..."

The section states that failing to comply with the requirement, or giving false information, can be punished with up to two years imprisonment if tried on indictment or, if tried in a magistrates court, three months imprisonment or a fine.

It can be seen that this section faces a professional journalist or news photographer with a moral dilemma: does he follow the unwritten journalists' code of protecting his sources and face the threat of prosecution, or does he violate the code and reveal sources?

Further, in the case of an emergency, a chief officer may invoke Section 6 without obtaining the Home Secretary's permission providing he informs the Minister at a later date.

Search warrants, which normally have to be issued by a magistrate, are not needed under the Act in a case of emergency. Thus the police may enter premises and search and seize anything which may be relevant to an offence under the Act, without a warrant.

Defence Advisory Notices

Closely allied to the question of official secrets is the Defence Advisory (DA) Notices system operated by the Defence, Press and Broadcasting Committee. This committee is composed of representatives of the Government, press and broadcasting and is effectively a self-censorship system. The notices are issued after discussion by the committee and identify those areas considered to be dangerous and/or sensitive to state security. They also offer guidance on how matters subject to such a notice may be discussed, if at all.

These notices are distributed to the editors of national and provincial newspapers, radio and television companies, and publishers of periodicals and books which specialise in defence subjects.

The committee provides advice and guidance on matters which fall within the broad area of the DA Notices. The DA Notice secretariat is available to give advice to editors, defence correspondents and other journalists at all times and the telephone number is 0171-218 2206.

Currently there are six DA Notices and they cover:

1. Operations, plans and capabilities;
2. Non-nuclear weapons and operational equipment;
3. Nuclear weapons and equipment;
4. Ciphers and secure communications;
5. Identification of specific installations;
6. United Kingdom security and intelligence services.

The DA notices are not a blanket prohibition as such; they just describe what the notice is seeking to provide and why. The secretary of the Committee – always a retired high-ranking officer – will always discuss with editors, authors, publishers and programme makers more specific details of what may or may not be published.

He may even advise against further publication of information which may have been published already. The reason – a logical one – is that terrorists and/or other organisations which are hostile to this country often get their information from a variety of sources, which when pieced together can provide a composite and graphic picture of a particular subject.

An example of a DA Notice, which is printed here with the permission of the secretary of the Defence Press and Broadcasting Committee, is as follows:

OPERATIONS, PLANS AND CAPABILITIES

1. It is requested that disclosure or publication of highly classified information of the kind listed below should not be made without

first seeking advice:

(a) Details of present or future operations, methods, tactics and contingency planning to meet particular hostile situations and to counter threats of terrorist attacks;

(b) Details of the state of readiness and operational capability of individual units or formations whose involvement in such operations is current or may be imminent;

(c) Operational movements of such individual units or formations (as distinct from routine movements unconnected with operations);

(d) Particulars of current or projected tactics, trials, techniques and training (including anti-interrogation training and operational techniques and tactics used to counter terrorism);

(e) Details of defensive or counter-terrorist measures taken by individual installations, units or formations.

2. Rationale. It is important not to publish information which could be damaging to national security by giving a potential enemy important strategic or operational advantages which could be exploited by terrorists to devise counter-measures with the consequence that attacks which might otherwise be frustrated could prove successful, or could compromise counter-terrorist operations, endanger lives or put sources at risk.

7 Photography and the Legal System

The most well known court building in the country is the Old Bailey, or the Central Criminal Court to give it its correct name. Old Bailey is actually the street in the City of London where it stands, on the site of the old Newgate Prison. It has been photographed countless times and will continue to be of great interest to photographers for as long as it remains, doubtless for many, many years.

But photographers should note that it is, in fact, an offence under Section 41 of the *Criminal Justice Act 1925* to take any photograph, or make any portrait or sketch, in a court – and this restriction equally applies to photographs of persons entering or leaving a court or its precincts.

Photography in the courts

Unfortunately for photographers, there is no definition in the 1925 Act of what the precincts of a court actually are; they can be, in fact, anything the court decides – within reason.

Press photographers who cover the courts are fully aware of the rules against taking photographs inside a court or its precincts and take every care to ensure that, when taking photographs of anyone involved in a case either entering or leaving a court, the court building itself is not shown.

So it is the enthusiastic amateur or foreign news photographer who is most likely to fall foul of the law in this respect.

In many of the major cities of England and Wales, courts are held in fine historic buildings which are worthy of a photograph in their own right. Nothing could make a better picture than a High Court judge in his red robes and retinue entering or leaving the court. But to take such a photograph is inviting trouble, as an amateur photographer discovered in Nottingham some years ago. He was promptly arrested, brought before the judge, and fined!

On the other hand, during the A6 murder trial at Bedford Assizes in 1961, a *cause celebre* whose echoes are heard even today, the late Mr Justice Gorman fully appreciated the reality of the situation. He agreed with photographers and cameramen that they could, on one occasion only, photograph and/or film him leaving the court to go to his lodgings.

This was a sensible approach which was respected and observed by those photographers and cameramen attending the trial.

It is not uncommon for a judge to leave a court to take evidence from a witness in hospital, or to visit a location which plays an important role in a trial, be it either civil or criminal. In these circumstances professional photographers and cameramen know that an approach to the judge's clerk for guidance will often result in a positive reply, even though there may be qualifications – the most important of which is most likely to be a ban on photographing the jury.

As suggested above, it is the photographer who is unaware of the law who is most likely to get into trouble, especially those working for foreign publications and perhaps covering a major trial in this country for the first time. During the trial of Peter Sutcliffe, the "Yorkshire Ripper", at the Old Bailey, a photographer for a German magazine took a photograph inside the courtroom, using sophisticated equipment so that his action went unnoticed.

When the photograph was published and the publication brought to the notice of the judge, the London editor of the magazine was banned from attending the remainder of the trial.

Contempt of court

The greatest risk of legal action following publication of photographs comes from contempt of court, when publication is likely to create a substantial risk that the course of justice in a particular judicial proceeding will be seriously prejudiced or impaired. To understand the rationale behind the situation of a publication being in contempt of court, a look at the historical background will be of help.

Until quite recently contempt was a common law offence; that is an offence created not by Act of Parliament but by custom, usage and decisions of courts going back many centuries. As far as publishing contempt is concerned, it consists, in the main, of actions likely to impair the course of justice.

In most cases publication of a photograph will only constitute contempt if the question of the identity of an accused is likely to be an issue in a forthcoming trial.

In 1927 the *Daily Mirror* was held to be in common law contempt for publishing a photograph of an accused person on the morning of the day he was due to appear on an identity parade. Lord Hewart, the then Lord Chief Justice, observed that there was a duty to refrain from publication where it was apparent to a reasonable man that the question of identity in a trial would arise.

Many years later, when the then Young Liberal activist Peter Hain was arrested and charged with robbing a bank, the London *Evening Standard* published a photograph of him under the heading: "I'm no bank robber." This was held to be a contempt, as a question of identity arose. In the event Peter Hain was rightly acquitted.

Contempt in Scotland

It is in Scotland that there have been several decisions in the not too distant past, concerning contempt of court by publication of photographs. Scotland has a different legal system to that which obtains in England and Wales, embodying principles drawn from Roman law and common law.

For the purpose of this chapter it is only necessary to look at Scottish decisions which have been accepted as being much tougher than those made under English law.

In 1960 the *Scottish Daily Mail* was fined £5,000 and its editor £500 for publishing an article about a double murderer. As a result of the judgment of Lord Clyde in that case, Scottish newspapers felt themselves very much restricted as far as what they could publish once police were investigating a crime. In the same year the Glasgow-based *Daily Record* was fined £7,500 and the editor £500, for publishing the photograph of a footballer who had been arrested on charges of indecency.

Perhaps more significantly, a photograph figured in a case in 1978 against London Weekend Television. LWT and three executives were fined a total of £61,000 for contempt after screening a photograph of a nursing sister and referring to her trial which was due to start the following day at Edinburgh Sheriff Court. The interesting point is that the indictment against the nursing sister was dropped.

In the hearing of the case against LWT, Lord Emslie, Scotland's Lord Justice General as he then was, said there was no difficulty in accepting that there was no hard and fast rule that publication of an accused's photograph would always be contempt. He added, however, that a photograph of an accused would only constitute contempt where a question of identity had or might arise, and where publication of the photograph was calculated to prejudice the prospect of a fair trial.

Although such a ruling would be persuasive rather than binding on an English court, it confirmed what had been the basis of what may be termed "photographic contempt" in England and Wales: that there is no contempt in publishing the photograph of an accused person unless identity is in dispute.

The Contempt of Court Act 1981

Another reason for the contempt rule as far as publishing photographs of an accused person before their trial is concerned, is that the fact that the photograph has been published could well influence a witness to positively identify the accused when, without that photograph, identification may not have taken place at all, or with some uncertainty and qualification.

And it must not be assumed that prejudice applies only to the defence in a criminal court – it can apply equally well to publication of anything which might affect the case for the prosecution.

Greater certainty now exists under the *Contempt of Court Act 1981* which, during its passage through Parliament, was claimed by the Government to be a piece of legislation which would reform and liberalise common law contempt. However, despite the Act, common law contempt can still be committed.

Under the Act any writing, speech or broadcast can be treated as contempt regardless of intent if it creates a substantial risk that the course of justice in the proceedings in question – civil as well as criminal – will be seriously prejudiced. The Act also introduced the principle of proceedings having to be "active" before a contempt can be committed.

Proceedings are deemed to be active in criminal cases if a person has been arrested or a warrant for arrest or a summons to appear in court has been issued. However, there is a defence if, at the time of publication and having taken all reasonable care, the editor, writer or publisher did not know and had no reason to suspect that proceedings were active.

In criminal cases proceedings cease to be active if:

A person has not been arrested within twelve months of a warrant being issued;

An arrested person has been released without being charged, although this would not be the case if that person had been released on police bail;

The case is discontinued, the defendant is found to be unfit to be tried or unfit to plead, or the court orders the charge to lie on the file;

Where the accused is acquitted or sentenced.

Frequently sentence is postponed after a conviction for social reports. Strictly speaking, the risk of contempt still exists, for the accused has yet to be sentenced. But it is generally thought that publication of a background piece, which may or may not include photographs, is unlikely to influence a judge in his sentencing.

Proceedings would be reactivated if an appeal is lodged. The risk of contempt runs from the time the appeal is officially lodged, but not before, even if a defence lawyer announces in open court that an appeal is to be lodged.

It is generally assumed that there will be no contempt in England and Wales in publishing a photograph as long as identification is not in issue, but of course it may not be until the end of a trial that this fact is finally established.

Photographs of a crime

From time to time a photographer may be in a position to take photographs of a crime actually being committed. Very often this is in the case of crowd violence at a football match or a major demonstration.

Would publication of such photographs constitute contempt of court? It is submitted that the answer must be no, always provided that the photographs have not been published with a caption which suggests the persons depicted are guilty of some crime.

Provided the photographs have not been tampered with they are of course evidence of the crime being committed. In the event of a trial the photographs would in all probability be placed before a court as "best evidence", with the photographer being called to testify to the fact that he took the pictures.

If the photograph(s) could be capable of bearing two interpretations it is for prosecuting and defence counsel to prove to the jury by means of other evidence whether the photograph(s) bear the meaning each lawyer would wish them to bear. Publication of such photographs would only be likely to constitute contempt if accompanied by an article or caption making a positive assertion that those depicted are guilty.

Police access to photographs

In 1984 the *Police and Criminal Evidence Act* (PACE) came into effect. For the first time it gave the police the power to have access to material which they consider would be of substantial value in investigating a serious arrestable offence, and would be likely to provide relevant evidence in such investigations.

An arrestable offence is one where the penalty on first conviction can be at least five years imprisonment or, in the case of murder, where the penalty is fixed by statute. Taking a car without authority or driving with excess of alcohol or drugs in the blood are also arrestable offences even though the penalties are less than five years imprisonment.

Furthermore, a police officer may arrest without a warrant if he suspects a person of having committed an arrestable offence.

Under PACE the police can apply to a circuit judge for an order giving them access to what the Act describes as "journalistic material". PACE defines journalistic material as material "acquired or created for the purpose of journalism." However, the particular target for such an order has to be given the opportunity to resist the application in court.

There are two safeguards available to the media – excluded material and special procedure material.

In the case of excluded material the police can obtain an order only if they had power under the old law to obtain a search warrant – if the material had been stolen – or if an offence under the *Official Secrets Act* was suspected. Excluded material includes journalistic material held in confidence and consisting of documents or records.

Special procedure material includes material not held in confidence, such as photographs, and a judge can make an order giving the police access to such material if he rules it is in the public interest so to do. As far as special procedure material is concerned most, if not all, of what cases there have been under the Act have indeed referred to photographs.

Following riots in the St Paul's area of Bristol in 1986 the police sought untransmitted television newsreel footage from two television companies, and unpublished news photographs taken by freelance picture agency photographers as well as staff photographers employed by the *Bristol Evening Post* and *Western Daily Press*.

Having been refused, the police applied to a judge at Bristol Crown Court for an order under the Act. This was granted, although the judge did not ask the police to specify offences which had been committed, nor the relevance or the probative value of the material required. The police asked for 190 photographs and all the television footage taken between specific times during the rioting.

In opposition it was argued in vain that to grant the police request would not be in the public interest since it would compromise the impartiality of the media and endanger photographers and television cameramen if those participating in offences knew that such an order could be made. Nevertheless, the judge ruled that the public interest in catching those suspected of committing a crime outweighed these arguments.

Although this case applied to the professional media, it is not beyond the realms of probability that an amateur photographer who took similar photographs or video footage could be forced to hand over prints, negatives or tapes to the police.

Following anti-poll tax riots in and around London's Trafalgar Square in 1990, an application was made by the Metropolitan Police for the handing over of pictures of the event. During the course of the hearings, news organisations submitted that the application by the police was premature, as they had not yet examined all material handed to them by many other organisations. The judge ruled that until the police had seen the material they could not tell whether or not it was relevant.

On a previous occasion, in 1987, following disturbances during a demonstration at Wapping to mark the anniversary of a strike by employees of News International, a judge made an order for film and photographs to be handed over. Four freelance photographers did not comply, but they were held not to be in contempt of court since the photographs were no longer in their hands, having been sent to the Brussels headquarters of the International Federation of Journalists. However, when a film maker making a production for Channel 4 claimed that material had been sent out of the jurisdiction of the court, this defence was not accepted.

Under PACE the police can apply to a judge for a search warrant and any organ of the media or, indeed, an individual photographer, does not have the right to be heard. But if this step is taken the judge must be satisfied that not only the criteria already referred to exists – the arrestable offence etc – but that one of a number of circumstances apply.

These circumstances are if:

It is not practicable to communicate with anyone entitled to grant entry to the premises;

It is not practicable to communicate with anyone entitled to grant access to the material;

That the material contains information which is subject to an obligation of secrecy or a restriction on disclosure by statute – as would be material subject to the *Official Secrets Act* – and is likely to be disclosed in breach of that obligation if a search warrant is not issued;

That serving a notice of an order to produce might seriously prejudice an investigation of a crime.

Reporting restrictions

There are no restrictions on naming defendants or witnesses in cases in Magistrates Courts or Crown Courts, although there are exceptions to this as far photographs are concerned. But in cases which are committed for trial from magistrates courts – unless reporting restrictions are lifted – details of a report are limited to

the ten following points:
  1. Name of court and of the examining magistrate or justices;
  2. Name(s), address(es) and occupations of parties and witnesses and the age of defendant(s) and witnesses;
  3. The offence(s) with which the defendant(s) is charged or a summary of them;
  4. Names of solicitors and counsel in the proceedings;
  5. The decision of the court to commit for trial and the decisions on any defendant(s) not committed;
  6. Charges on which the defendant(s) is committed or a summary of them and the court to which committed;
  7. The date and place to which the committal is adjourned;
  8. Any arrangements as to bail on adjournment or committal;
  9. Whether legal aid was granted;
  10. Any decision of the court to lift or not lift reporting restrictions.

These restrictions do not apply if a defendant successfully applies to the court to have them lifted or if the accused is not committed for trial. If a court trying one or more defendants decides to try one summarily, the Act allows evidence to be reported in the case of that person being tried even if the evidence also impinges on the case of those who are being sent for trial.

Restrictions do not apply where a court commits an accused to a Crown court for sentence, because he has already been tried. And of course they do not apply when the defendant(s) has been tried at a Crown court.

This is unlikely to be a situation the average photographer would ever have to deal with, but it is one which media photographers frequently face in their day-to-day work. Knowledge of these restrictions is important, especially in these days of "multi-skilling" where photographers may be expected to write a report, or reporters to take photographs.

Most important for the media photographer is to be aware that publication of a photograph of an accused person(s) could well be, as emphasised earlier in this chapter, a contempt of court if identity is likely to be an issue.

It must also be remembered that there are circumstances where a witness cannot be identified, which means a photograph of that witness cannot be published. One instance would be if an order under Section 11 of the *Contempt of Court Act 1981* is made. This allows a court to ban the publication of the name of a witness – and obviously this includes a photograph. This is a power which the courts only invoke in rare cases, usually where the witness is a member of the SAS or the security services, or is the victim of blackmail for which the accused is being tried.

Sexual offences

the *Sexual Offences (Amendment) Act 1976* prohibited the publication of anything which would identify the defendant (unless he was convicted) or the complainant in any proceedings for rape, attempted rape, or aiding, abetting, counselling and procuring rape. Although under the Act only a man can commit rape or attempted rape, a woman can be convicted of counselling, procuring, aiding or abetting the offence.

This legislation was amended by the *Criminal Justice Act 1988* which added two more offences subject to restrictions – conspiracy to rape and burglary with intent to rape – and also lifted the shield of anonymity from the defendant who can be named in connection with these offences and, subject to any other restrictions which might apply relating to contempt or identification of juveniles, can also be identified by way of a published photograph.

The anonymity to victims is enforced through the *Sexual Offences (Amendment) Act 1992*, which also extended the protection of anonymity not just to victims of those rape offences already outlined but other sexual offences. The *Criminal Justice and Public Order Act 1994* extended this protection to victims of male rape.

The restrictions on identifying the complainant apply in two stages. Once an allegation of rape has been made either by the victim or some other person, the victim's name, address and picture must not be published in his or her lifetime if it is likely to identify them as a victim of the offence. And after a person has been accused of a rape or other sexual offence no material – and this includes photographs – likely to led to identification of the victim or complainant must be published during his or her lifetime.

There are exceptions to this. One is if a judge decides that the veil of anonymity imposes a substantial and unreasonable restriction on the reporting of a trial and he considers it in the public interest to raise the prohibition. The judge may also lift the ban if a defendant successfully applies for it to be lifted in an attempt to bring witnesses forward without whom the defence would be substantially prejudiced.

Publication of a complainant's name – and by extension, photograph – does not apply in a report of criminal proceedings where a person is charged with offences other than those mentioned. It would definitely cover the situation where someone has made a false allegation of rape or related offences and has been charged with either perjury or wasting police time.

Nor do the restrictions apply in the case of a victim consenting in writing to being identified, though that consent will be vitiated if it is obtained by interfering with their peace or comfort.

It must also be remembered that anonymity also covers civil proceedings for damages for rape, or hearings where allegations of rape are made at an industrial tribunal.

The other sexual offences for which the 1992 Act permitted anonymity to be granted to the complainant are as follows:

Intercourse with a mentally handicapped person;
Indecent conduct towards young children;
Incitement to commit incest with a granddaughter, daughter or sister who is under the age of 16;
Intercourse with a girl under 13 or between the age of 13 and 16;
Procurement of a woman by threats or false pretences;
Administering drugs to obtain intercourse;
Procurement of a mentally handicapped person;
Incest by a man or woman;
Indecent assault on either a man or woman;
Buggery and assault with intent to commit buggery.

The Act defines a complainant as the person against whom the offence is said to have been committed.

Again, restrictions may be lifted by a magistrate either at a summary trial or by a judge at a Crown court if the judge is satisfied they impose a substantial and unreasonable restriction on reporting the proceedings or if lifting the prohibition on identity will help in tracing witnesses for the defence.

One of the major problems faced by the media when reporting rape and/or sexual offences is what has become known as "jigsaw" identification. For example, if the accused is related to or can be linked to the complainant, newspapers may name the accused – or if identity is not in issue publish his photograph – while making sure that there is nothing that could possible identify the complainant. The problem can arise when there are two newspapers published in the area, or a newspaper and a local radio station.

It may well be that the accused person, who can be identified, is charged with an offence against his wife – as rape can now exist within marriage – or even his daughter. If one paper and/or radio station named the accused but failed to say that the offence concerned his wife or daughter that would be all well and good; the problem would arise if another paper or radio station did not name the accused in its reports, but said he was charged with an offence against his wife or daughter. Thus it would not be difficult for people exposed to both media outlets to put two and two together and come to the conclusion that the accused's victim was his wife or his daughter.

In order to avoid these problems the former Press Council urged editors to co-operate and follow the same policy as to how the case is reported, so that jigsaw identification does not arise. Under the code of practice issued by the Press Complaints Commission (which replaced the Press Council) it is suggested that newspapers should not publish material likely to contribute to the identification of victims of sexual attack unless they are free by law to do so. Where children are concerned the Press Complaints Commission say that the involved adult should not be identified and nothing which is reported should suggest the relationship between the accused and the victim.

Youth courts

Since the publication of the last edition of this book there have been developments relating to what was once known as juvenile courts.

The two main Acts which govern reporting of children in the news – and this includes, of course, publication of photographs – are the *Children Act 1989* and the *Children and Young Persons Act 1933*. Juvenile courts, established under the 1933 Act, were renamed youth courts in 1992, and the age limit of 17 was raised to 18.

Section 47 of the 1933 Act bars the public from attending youth courts, but *bona fide* representatives of newspapers and news agencies are permitted to attend. This would include photographers employed by the media although, of course, they are banned from taking photographs.

Section 49 of the 1933 Act states that reports from these courts must not contain anything which would lead to a juvenile being identified. There is a specific ban on photographs, and this includes not only the accused but also a juvenile as complainant or as witness. It is not a bar to a photograph being taken; the offence is publication of a photograph.

Similar restrictions apply to a juvenile appealing against a sentence and/or conviction, to a Crown court or to the Divisional court, on a point of law.

Curiously, restrictions against identifying a young person do not apply when he is tried with an adult at a magistrates court or at a Crown court, or appears at those courts as a witness. However, these courts do have the power under Section 39 of the 1933 Act to order that anything that may identify a juvenile appearing in proceedings should not be published. Newspapers, well aware of this anomaly in the law, quite often have house rules which result in a voluntary ban on identifying juveniles.

Magistrates in youth courts, and the Home Secretary, are empowered to lift restrictions on naming a young person, but only to avoid injustice to a particular individual.

Under the *Children Act 1989*, Section 97 makes it an offence to publish any material – and what could be a more positive means of identification than a photograph – that identified any child under 18 involved in family proceedings under the Act. This prohibition extends to reports on parents in dispute with social workers who are dealing with their (the parents') children.

Juvenile proceedings in Scotland

The situation in Scotland is somewhat different where juveniles are concerned. Since 1971 justice has been dispensed at Children's Hearings following the passing of the *Social Work (Scotland) Act 1968*. This abolished juvenile courts and instituted a system which was orientated towards the treatment of offenders. There is a bar to identification of children appearing at Children's Hearings, and also on persons up to the age of 18 if they are under a form of supervision imposed by one of the hearings.

But children who have committed certain crimes – murder, attempted murder, rape, assault to the danger of life, possession of offensive weapons, offences under the Road Traffic Acts for which disqualification from driving is a penalty, and offences where a child is charged with an adult – continue to be tried in the High Court or the Sheriff Court. This may be extended to a child who has committed an offence which, in the opinion of the prosecutor, merits prosecution in court in the public interest.

Nevertheless, no child appearing before a Children's Hearing, or hearings in a Sheriff Court or an appeal court, can be identified, and under the *Criminal Justice (Scotland) Act 1980* children appearing in criminal proceedings as either accused person(s), witnesses or victims, may not be identified. This ban does not apply if a person under 16 is a witness only, unless the court otherwise directs.

8 Public Places and Events

By the very nature of life, from time to time there are major disasters: air and train crashes, multiple pile-ups on a motorway, natural disasters such as floods and hurricanes and, regrettably today, terrorist activity.

It is at times like these – or what may best be described as occasions concerning the security of a particular person or persons – that photographers are likely to fall foul of the criminal law.

The risk of arrest

Cases are often reported of photographers being arrested either for obstruction or for behaviour likely to cause a breach of the peace. To the photographer concerned, the action of the police in these cases is seen as arbitrary at its best and dictatorial at its worst. Whenever a photographer is arrested while following his profession or hobby in recording events such as those described above, reason on both sides often seems to fly out of the window. But it is within the pages of a book such as this that the problem can be considered in a way which is devoid of emotion.

Subject to the restrictions on photography described in previous chapters, it is not an offence to take photographs of disasters or other major incidents. However, discretion should be observed at all times.

At a time of a major disaster or incident there is no doubt that both the police and rescue services have an onerous and thankless task to perform. Not only are they all part of the rescue operation, but the police in particular are also responsible for ensuring that such operations are carried out with the maximum of efficiency and the minimum of interference. It is regrettable that on many occasions photographers are seen as obstacles to be removed from the scene.

Consequently photographers are often unwittingly and unfairly cast in the role of minor villain, and the police show little sympathy with those who exercise their rights to take pictures. If arrests follow – and this applies not only to disasters but also to demonstrations or riots – the charge preferred is invariably that of behaviour which in London is charged under the *Metropolitan Police Act 1839* and in the rest of England and Wales under the *Public Order Act 1936*.

Under the former Act, it is an offence for any person to use words or behaviour with intent to provoke a breach of the peace or whereby a breach of the peace may be occasioned.

Under Section 5 of the *Public Order Act* as amended by the *Race Relations Act 1965* and Schedule 1 of the *Criminal Law Act 1977*, the wording is as follows:

"Any person who in any public place or at any public meeting uses threatening, abusive or insulting words or behaviour with intent to provoke a breach of the peace or whereby a breach of the peace is likely to be occasioned, shall be guilty of an offence..."

It is under this Act that photographers are most at risk when covering demonstrations or marches and this will be dealt with first.

Public gatherings

There is no doubt that members of many extremist organisations at both ends of the political spectrum dislike being photographed taking part in marches or demonstrations. Consequently, a photographer, merely by pointing his camera at such people, can either cause a breach of the peace or be likely to do so.

In principle, to be an offence an action must be more than one calculated to cause annoyance. What is unfortunate in these circumstances is that many policemen, anxious to preserve the peace, take a subjective rather than an objective view of photographers' actions. They assume, sometimes incorrectly, that a breach of the peace is most likely. The photographer is therefore arrested, and then has the unenviable task of persuading magistrates that his action did not, or was unlikely to, cause a breach of the peace.

Under the Act the penalty on conviction is imprisonment for no more than six months and/or a fine.

It must be stressed that this offence is most likely to be charged under the *Public Order Act* which is far more draconian in terms of punishment than the much earlier *Metropolitan Police Act*.

Other incidents

It is under the *Metropolitan Police Act* – or similar legislation for the rest of the country – that a photographer is likely to be charged at the scene of a disaster or major terrorist incident.

Only a few years ago a cameraman was arrested and convicted under just such a provision for persisting in taking a photograph of an Army officer defusing a bomb that had been placed by the IRA. The reasoning behind this particular arrest was that the officer had protested at having his photograph taken because of possible reprisals against himself or his family if he was identified.

There is no doubt that in circumstances like this, or during any disaster or a major incident, photographers could unintentionally get in the way of the police and/or rescue workers. This could eventually lead to a heated exchange of words or even blows being struck.

In 1995 a BBC news cameraman was arrested after filming scenes of a coach crash involving a number of students. Police told the magistrates that the cameraman had been arrested because he had refused to leave the scene of the accident in what, according to the police, was a highly charged situation, and because they (the police) feared for the cameraman's safety. He was subsequently bound over to keep the peace by magistrates in Bangor, Wales.

The cameraman appealed. When the appeal was heard at the local Crown court, prosecuting counsel said the case was not about whether or not it was reasonable for TV news to record and show distressing scenes, but that the cameraman was himself the cause of the distress.

Allowing the appeal the circuit judge, hearing the case with magistrates, said there was no real risk of repetition of the offence and that the conduct of the cameraman was on its own insufficient to uphold the original decision of the magistrates. However, the judge went on to say that he believed the cameraman had acted with excessive enthusiasm and added: "It's as well to remember that others have feelings and rights too."

Not unnaturally the police seek to obviate circumstances such as those outlined above, or any incidents which may impede rescue workers, and one way they do this is to arrest photographers or cameramen. Again it must be remembered that it is not necessary for a breach of the peace to take place; it is only necessary for there to be a likelihood of such an event happening.

Railways present a difficult proposition – it is an offence under a number of statutes appertaining to railways, going back to the *Railway Regulation Act 1840*, to wilfully obstruct or impede any agent or officer of the railway in the execution of his duty, or to wilfully trespass on the railway itself, stations, works or premises. It is worth noting in this respect that it is not only when photographing railway accidents that a photographer is at risk. There are other occasions when a photographer may find himself technically committing trespass for the sake of a dramatic photograph, especially if the subject of such a photograph should involve taking it from a railway cutting or some other place on land which belongs to the railway.

Obstruction

Another arm of the law which the police can and do use with success is to arrest photographers who do not move on when ordered to do so. These cases can lead to other charges in which the word "obstruction" figures prominently.

Section 121 of the *Highways Act 1959* provides that if a person without lawful authority or excuse in any way wilfully obstructs the free passage of a highway he is guilty of an offence.

The word "wilful" has a multitude of meanings but can generally be assumed to mean the exercise of free will, which would surely be the case as far as a photographer is concerned.

The other offence in which the word obstruction is used in the charge is a more serious one and is likely to be brought against a photographer who persists in taking photographs and argues with a policeman. "Any person who resists or wilfully obstructs a constable in the execution of his duty ... shall be guilty of an offence ", under Section 51 of the *Police Act 1964*.

A photographer charged with this offence may find it more difficult to mount a defence, as the meaning of "wilful" in this instance was decided in 1977 to mean an intention to obstruct an officer in the sense of making it more difficult for him to do his job. It is not difficult to see how a harassed policeman at the scene of an incident may well think a photographer refusing to move on or arguing is making it more difficult for him (the officer) to carry out his duties. But unsurprisingly there are times when the police are guilty of overreaction.

Early in 1995, while covering an animal rights demonstration about the export of calves to the continent, a photographer with an East Anglian news agency was arrested as he took photographs of police advancing on protesters who were blocking the road by sitting down. Despite repeatedly explaining that he had done nothing wrong and trying to show his press card, and the fact that other newsmen and members of the crowd were shouting that he was indeed a press photographer, he was put in a police van where he was held for an hour before being taken to a police station.

There he continued to protest his innocence and told police that his camera contained films which were urgently required by newspapers. He was finally informed that he would be allowed to go without being charged if he signed a caution form, which is tantamount to admitting an offence.

He refused, and although his employer faxed the Chief Constable pointing out that a mistake had been made he was not released on police bail until he had been detained for nine hours. Eventually, after being charged with wilful obstruction of the highway, he was found not guilty by magistrates. At the time of writing he is suing the police for wrongful arrest and false imprisonment and is claiming for the £1,200 legal costs he incurred in proving his innocence. Despite clearing him the magistrates refused to award costs against the police.

Incidents of the type discussed do not always occur on public land; they frequently happen on land which is privately owned and here the photographer is on safer ground. Provided he has permission to be on the land a photographer – although still liable to arrest for obstruction or insulting behaviour – cannot legally be asked to move on. He has permission to be on the land and his rights in this respect are discussed in a later chapter.

Rights and remedies

The above is a formidable list of traps for photographers. But there are counterbalances to be found, mostly in civil law, which are based on old established rights created over the centuries to protect the person and the property of an individual.

For the purpose of this part of the chapter it is assumed the photographer is not trespassing, nor obstructing a constable in the execution of his duty or using behaviour which could occasion a breach of the peace.

Perhaps the most drastic remedy which could be brought against a constable, or any other person who unlawfully restrains a citizen of this country or even a foreign visitor, is the tort of false imprisonment.

A tort is a civil wrong and the law broadly recognises that for every wrong there is a legal remedy. There are two distinctions here: *Injuria* is a legal concept which means an injury having legal consequences, and this is distinguished from *damnum*, which is the damage suffered.

The two do not always go together as it is possible for a person to suffer damage without having a legal remedy; to claim for harm done there must be a violation of a legal right. Even an act done with malice to another does not give rise to a cause of action unless a legal right is violated.

False imprisonment

False imprisonment is the unauthorised bodily restraint of a person without lawful authority. Such a situation could arise, as far as a photographer is concerned, when either a constable, official or even an ordinary citizen, restrains the photographer's movements. It is not necessary for a person to be imprisoned in the popular sense of being locked up.

The essence of this tort is that the restriction of a person's freedom of movement must be absolute. Thus a photographer who is restricted from continuing in a forward direction towards, say, the scene of an incident, would not have a case if he is free to move in another direction, even if it is not the way he wishes to go.

On the other hand if the photographer was to find himself in an alleyway with a dead-end between high buildings and with his only way out barred, he would have a strong case for false imprisonment as his freedom of movement is then absolutely restrained in the sense that he cannot leave the alleyway.

Cases of false imprisonment are a rarity, although it is possible to think of situations analogous to the one discussed which photographers may have faced in the past or may well encounter in the future.

Assault

It is most likely that a photographer would seek to enforce his rights for any injury he may have suffered. This would be via an action for assault and/or battery, but it must be remembered that there has to be a legal cause of action. Being jostled in a crowd is insufficient to sustain a claim for assault and/or battery as the law presumes that, by joining a crowd, a person consents to any jostling that may follow.

There is a difference in law between assault and battery: assault, contrary to what most people think, is not striking a blow which actually lands on a person. It is an attempt or threat to apply such force which constitutes the tort of assault. The situation must be such that the person offering violence is in a position to carry out the threat and puts the person to whom it is offered in fear of such violence.

At one time it was considered that the mere utterance of a threat would not constitute assault, but in *Ansell v Thomas (1974)* the Court of Appeal held that a threat to use force was sufficient to found an action for assault.

Assault is not only a tort – a civil wrong – it is also a crime. A person on conviction can be fined and/or imprisoned for common or simple assault, with longer terms for assaults of a more serious nature.

Battery is the intention to bring any material object onto the person of another, provided there is sufficient use of force to give rise to battery.

It is interesting to note that some academic lawyers have put forward the proposition that the unauthorised taking of a photograph with a flash might be considered battery, because the projection of throwing the sharp light from a flash, causing personal discomfort, would constitute this tort. This view may well have greater significance now, following a recent decision that a stalker was guilty of causing grievous bodily harm even though that harm was mental rather than physical.

Before photographers consider bringing an action for assault and/or battery, they or their legal advisers will no doubt consider the defences available to the person to be sued, one of the most important of which is that of self-defence.

This defence extends to the protection of those a person has the moral or legal obligation to protect. It is possible that a person seeking to avoid publicity for himself and his family would resort to assault or battery to avoid any exposure that publication of a photograph would bring. Indeed, it need not be to avoid publicity; the situation could arise from a street photographer whose persistence is causing embarrassment, or even a person taking a candid shot. Whether in such cases self-defence would be a valid defence to a civil action would depend on the circumstances of the individual case.

What must be remembered is that a photographer, or any other person, who wishes to be recompensed for any harm suffered, should not bring an action in the magistrates court. Under Sections 44-45 of the *Offences Against the Persons Act 1861*, if a summary prosecution is launched and a person is convicted and punished, even if that punishment is no more than an absolute discharge, no further action or civil proceedings may be taken in respect of that particular incident. Similarly, if the case is dismissed and magistrates issue a certificate of dismissal, any further action is barred.

Trespass to the person by way of assault and/or battery is not actionable in itself; to successfully sustain such an action the plaintiff has to prove either negligence and/or intention on the part of the defendant. This is a matter of fact rather than of law.

Damages which may be awarded will vary from case to case and the greater the injury suffered, the higher the damages are likely to be. If a case for false imprisonment is successful, aggravated damages may be awarded for any humiliation the plaintiff has suffered, as well as ordinary damages.

Interference with camera or film

It is not uncommon for photographers to have their cameras seized and damaged, or handed back with the film ripped out. When this happens another tort arises, that of trespass to goods – although the permanent witholding of a camera or film is, of course, theft, and a criminal offence.

In most cases however, any civil action is likely to be accompanied by the tort of trespass to the person, for the very act of seizing the camera is likely to be accompanied by an assault and/or battery. The *Torts (Interference with Goods) Act 1977* defines wrongful interference as including any trespass to goods, conversion of goods, negligence or any other act which results in damage to goods or to a person's interest in goods.

For the purpose of discussing wrongful interference with goods by trespass, it will be assumed that the photographer is either the owner of the camera or has the legal right to have it in his possession, for the right of possession has to exist at the time the wrongful interference is committed. The plaintiff must also prove a direct interference with the goods, but this would not be difficult in a case where the camera is seized or even just pushed aside, for the interference is self-evident.

The problem a photographer faces in bringing an action for trespass to goods is the question of the quantum of damages to be recovered. If a camera is damaged or a film ripped out, the question of quantum is not difficult: it is the value of the repair, or of the film, or both. Where the problem really begins to bite is quantifying the value of the pictures taken on the destroyed or removed film, or those which would have been taken if the camera had not been damaged.

If what was depicted on the destroyed or damaged film was either a newsworthy incident or a picture of artistic merit, both of which were capable of commanding payment if published or exhibited, this must be taken into account in any claim for damages. But the photographer will have to demonstrate to the court that had he not been stopped by damage to the camera and/or film, the photographs would have been worth a particular sum of money to him.

To prove this it would be necessary for the photographer to produce evidence of what a particular publication or other outlet would have paid for the photographs, or what their earnings might be from sales by other means. However, no difficulty would arise if the photographer had been commissioned to take the photographs and a specific fee had been agreed.

An intriguing point arises when consideration is given to the case of the commissioned photographer referred to in the previous paragraph, or the photographer employed by a newspaper or magazine and assigned to photograph a newsworthy incident. In both instances the photographer loses nothing himself; the commissioned freelance may well receive his agreed fee in all the circumstances, while the staff photographer has suffered no monetary loss by not getting photographs.

If, as a result of damage to the camera and/or film, the newspaper or magazine has suffered a loss of circulation – difficult if not impossible to prove – or of syndication fees as the result of not getting the photograph(s), they must have a cause of action because the photographer was acting on their behalf.

But here again it is necessary for the potential loss to be quantified. In such an ephemeral and intangible field as newsworthiness this might be difficult, although not impossible, to establish.

Claiming damages

The next question which arises in such circumstances is: who to sue?

If the person who has committed trespass to either the person and/or to goods is an individual, he or she is the person on whom a county court summons or High Court writ can be served. If the person is a servant (the legal term for an employee) or the agent of another individual or a company, and was acting in either of these capacities at the time of the trespass, both individual and the employer should be sued as the former can be said to be acting on the part of the latter.

Before 1947 the Crown enjoyed immunity from being sued for either tort or breach of contract, on the grounds of the old legal maxim that the King or Queen can do no harm. But in that year the *Crown Proceedings Act* was passed, with the result that the Crown – that is the Government – is now liable in the same way as any subject.

However, neither the Crown, or the authority which appoints or pays the police, are liable for torts committed by police officers. Section 48(1) of the *Police Act 1964* makes the chief officer of police for the area – or commissioner in those areas where the chief officer holds that title – liable for torts committed by his officers. The Act also provides for any damages and costs awarded against the chief officer of police to be paid out of police funds.

The legal options

Another question to be answered is what court to sue in. If damages claimed are what is known as liquidated – that is where the total amount sought to be recovered is known – or if they are unliquidated and the total of both claims is unlikely to be more than £3,000, then action may be brought in a small claims court. The limit for a personal injury claim is £1,000 – this is dealt with more fully in Chapter 15.

These courts are part of a county court and are presided over by a district judge. The whole proceedings are of an informal nature and more akin to arbitration. Although either side is allowed to be represented by a lawyer if they so wish, lawyers are discouraged as the winning litigant cannot claim his legal costs unless a difficult point of law is involved, which is most unlikely to be the case.

Any claim over £3,000 can be heard in either a county court or in the High Court, and for speed of process the county court is to be preferred especially as legal costs are lower in these courts than in the High Court. But the choice of court will invariably be dictated by the type of case and its complexity and is best left to the decision of a legal adviser.

Finally, what is meant by unliquidated or general damages? These are damages which can't be quantified, such as what, in monetary terms, is the value of pain or suffering suffered by the plaintiff as a result of an injury. Or, if a photographer is so seriously injured that he is unable to follow his hobby to the full extent to which he did before an accident, what is the loss of the enjoyment of his hobby worth in financial terms.

In other words, this covers the intangible effects of an accident or legal wrong a person has suffered. In many instances it is the intangibles involved in a damage claim that may lead a legal adviser to advise a client to bring an action in the High Court.

Harassment

Just before Parliament was dissolved in April of 1997 the Protection from Harassment Bill received the Royal assent and became an Act coming into effect from 1st May 1997. The Act, which was designed to prevent people from being harassed by stalkers, nuisance neighbours or racial abuse, created two new criminal offences.

At the higher level, one offence is where the person harassing another behaves in so threatening a manner that the victim fears for his safety. This carries a maximum penalty of five years imprisonment or an unlimited fine or both.

The second, lesser, offence is committed where the behaviour of the harasser, while not leading the victim to fear violence will be used against him, could nevertheless have a devastating effect on the victim. This offence is punishable by a maximum term of imprisonment of six months or a £5,000 fine or both.

For the offences to have been committed the behaviour must have occurred on at least two occasions. The offender does not have to have the intention to cause the victim to fear violence or feel harassed; all it is necessary for the prosecution to prove is that the conduct occurred in circumstances where a reasonable person would realise this would be the effect.

Both offences carry the power of arrest without a warrant and empower the police to search the harasser's property. Furthermore, a court hearing such a case will have the power to make a restraining order immediately after a person has been convicted. A breach of this order – to keep away from the victim – is also now a criminal offence with a maximum penalty of five years imprisonment or an unlimited fine or both.

The author believes it to be the view of the Home Office, from where the legislation emanated, that the Act was not envisaged to entrap photographers, especially media photographers, carrying out their legitimate work. But as there only have to be two occasions where a person can claim to be the intended victim of the lower level offence, a photographer who might be trying to get a photograph of a certain person could easily find himself arrested. If he appears in front of an unsympathetic bench of magistrates he could easily be convicted and become the subject of a restraining order.

Under the Act the victim of the lower level offence also has a civil remedy, which is to apply for an injunction to stop the behaviour complained of if such behaviour may cause stress in the future. A breach of this civil injunction would become a criminal offence carrying a maximum term of imprisonment of five years, an unlimited fine or both.

During the summer of 1996 the Princess of Wales gained an injunction restraining a photographer, who had been in the practice of following her on his motorcycle, from approaching within 300 metres from her, communicating with her, harassing or interfering with her safety, security or wellbeing or molesting or assaulting her. Undoubtedly this incident played its part in speeding the Harassment Bill through Parliament.

The *Protection from Harassment Act*, which applies to England and Wales, contains provisions appropriate to the law in Scotland. There is a defence to both the criminal and civil measures that the "harassment" is carried out on the grounds of national security, the prevention or detection of an offence, and that the harasser is acting under statutory authority, and – in respect of the lesser offence only – the course of conduct complained of in the particular circumstances is reasonable.

It may be true that according to the Home Office the Act was not envisaged to trap photographers, but as will be seen in the next chapter, the *Criminal Justice and Public Order Act 1994*, which was aimed at dealing with, *inter alia*, "New Age travellers", and created the offence of aggravated trespass, has already caught some journalists and a press photographer – although they were all subsequently acquitted.

Within days of the new Act receiving the Royal assent, a bizarre incident involving the Princess of Wales, an award-winning Royal photographer and a passer-by, was played out outside a gymnasium in West London.

According to a report in *The Times*, the photographer took a picture of the Princess from 50 feet away and was astonished when the Princess ran across the road, demanded the film, and then called for help. This resulted in the passer-by (said to be a Gaelic footballer who makes his living as an hotel tout) stepping in, forcing the photographer against a wall, putting an arm lock on him and removing the film from the photographer's camera.

All this was captured on film by another freelance photographer who was reported to have sold his pictures for about £8,000. The picture published in *The Times* certainly showed force being used. Later the Princess issued a statement expressing the hope that the *Protection from Harassment Act* "will give greater protection to people such as herself who are the victims of this kind of distressing intrusion into their private lives."

But it was also reported that legal sources doubted whether the Princess would win a prosecution under the Act. Although no reasons were given for this view, from what was reported of the incident this was a one-off situation and, as has been noted, at least two instances are necessary for a conviction.

The police were reported to be "furious" and said it demonstrated the need for the Princess to have her full-time police protection restored. They added: "Apart from anything else, an alleged assault took place, and a theft."

However there was no action taken because the photographer made no complaint.

9   Privacy and Private Property

Unlike the situation which obtains in the United States of America and in some European countries such as France, in this country there is no right to privacy which is specifically protected by law.

Of course there is no greater intruder into privacy than the camera, and this is particularly true today with the ever increasing sophistication of zoom lenses which enable a photographer to take pictures from a distance. But having said there is no specific law giving a person a right to privacy, there are a number of other laws which afford some protection and of which photographers should have some knowledge.

Trespass

Earlier reference has been made to the problems photographers can face by trespassing. Unauthorised entry on another person's land is a trespass and is actionable *per se*. It is not necessary for actual damage to the land to be proved, although any damages awarded as a result of a legal action are likely to be nominal.

There can be instances when photographers are given permission to go onto another's land to take photographs but become trespassers if, when asked to leave, they do not do so. In those circumstances, the landowner is entitled to use reasonable force to eject the trespasser.

Similarly, when a photographer is invited into a person's house or onto his land for a specific purpose and then does something contrary to or in excess of that purpose, the photographer becomes what is known as a trespasser *ab initio* – a legal term which means "from the beginning". In other words, an act contrary to the purpose for which the invitation to enter was given, may lead to a case of trespass.

It is media photographers who are most likely to find themselves guilty of trespassing *ab initio*. They may often be invited into premises to discuss the taking of photographs of a particular individual or individuals who are currently newsworthy. If that person or persons decline to be photographed it is not unknown for a picture to be "snatched".

But from the moment that this is done the photographer becomes a trespasser; he was invited onto the premises simply to discuss the possibility of taking photographs and for no other reason. The unauthorised taking of a photograph is sufficient to revoke the licence which a court would imply was granted to enter for the discussion. The licence is automatically revoked by the wrongful act and the photographer becomes a trespasser from the time he entered.

However, it should be remembered that there is no right to confiscate the film in such circumstances as the photographer – even when trespassing – or his employer, retains copyright in the photographs and right to possession of the film.

Aggravated trespass

Reference has already been made to the *Criminal Justice and Public Order Act 1994*, which created the criminal offence of aggravated trespass. Although the intention of Parliament was, it is understood by the author, to give police the necessary powers to deal with what are called "New Age travellers" or others assembling for impromptu rock concerts or demonstrations, it could be used against media photographers.

Basically the offence is committed if a person trespasses on land in the open air and, to quote the Act, "...in relation to any lawful activity which persons are engaging in or about to engage in on that or adjoining land in the open air..." does something of an intimidating nature so as to deter them from engaging in that activity, or obstructs or disrupts that activity. For the purpose of this offence, highways and roads are excluded from the definition of land. A person can be arrested without a warrant and on conviction can be imprisoned for up to three months and/or fined.

The Act states that if a senior police officer has reason to believe that a person is committing, has committed or intends to commit the offence of aggravated trespass, or that two or more persons are trespassing on land with the common purpose of intimidating persons so as to deter, obstruct or disrupt a lawful activity, he may either himself, or authorise a constable, to direct those people to leave.

Failure to leave as soon as practicable or, having left, re-entering the land as a trespasser within a period of three months from the day the direction to leave was given, is also an offence with the same punishment referred to above.

It is not difficult to imagine a scenario where press photographers and TV cameramen are staking out a celebrity or a person who, for some reason or another, is in the news. They may be on land the owner of which they have been unable to contact to get permission – if they had even thought that necessary. It may even be the property of the person they are staking out – their front garden for example. Because of their presence, the person(s) whose land it is may be unable to make use of it for whatever reason they may wish to. That person could contact the local police station and lay a complaint of aggravated trespass.

It is even arguable that if photographers use a public park to maintain a photographic stake-out that the offence of aggravated trespass could be committed. A park is predominantly for pleasure purposes, and under bye-laws governing such places it is more than likely that there is a ban against the park being used for business or trade purposes. Who could argue that staking out a celebrity with the sole intention of getting photographs is not part of a trade or business?

Invasion of privacy

Aside from trespass further protection of privacy may be afforded by the laws of defamation, criminal libel, confidentiality and copyright – although these options can usually be invoked only after there has been an invasion of privacy. There is now also the more recent "harassment" legislation discussed in the previous chapter.

Over the years there have been many bodies which have looked into the question of privacy. As long ago as 1972 the Younger Committee on Privacy, set up by the Government of the day, rejected proposals that there should be a general remedy for the protection of privacy but recommended new remedies to cover certain specific ways in which privacy could be invaded. These recommendations were never implemented.

Within the last decade another Government appointed committee, under Sir David Calcutt QC, was set up to look at the question of privacy, or more specifically – breaches of privacy by the media. The Calcutt Committee made certain recommendations but again these proposals were never implemented by the government. However, Mr David Mellor, the then Government minister handling the matter, warned the press that they were "drinking at the Last Chance saloon."

Consequently those who seek to to enforce their right to privacy by use of other branches of the law continue to face a difficult task. This was amply demonstrated in 1977 in *Bernstein v Skyviews & General*. The plaintiff, Lord Bernstein, claimed damages for trespass to his land by the defendants, a firm of aerial photographers. Lord Bernstein claimed that by flying at the height of 630 feet over his land to take pictures of his home there had been a trespass.

The claim failed: Mr Justice Griffiths held that an owner of land did have, at common law, rights not only on and below his land, but also to the airspace above to such height as was necessary for his ordinary use and enjoyment of the land and anything on it. But he also held that even if the plane had flown over, it was too high to be considered to be trespassing. In any case, under Section 40(1) of the *Civil Aviation Act 1949*, there was a defence to such a claim against the operators of aircraft, where the height at which the aircraft was flying was considered reasonable.

However, Mr Justice Griffiths did add that constant surveillance from the air using photography might well be an actionable nuisance – an offence we shall discuss in more detail shortly.

The right to privacy

The question of whether or not there should be legislation providing a statutory right of privacy is, however, a topic that will not go away. It can be guaranteed to be resurrected whenever someone is "exposed" by the media for either imagined or real sins of omission or commission.

However, there are some lawyers who argue that a law of privacy already exists. They point to a judicial finding of the House of Lords – the highest court in the land – in the case of *Morris v Beardmore 1980*, and quote from the judgment of Lord Scarman.

In his judgment Lord Scarman described the right of privacy as fundamental. He did this, he explained, for two reasons: "First, it is apt to describe the importance attached by the common law to the privacy of the home... second, the right enjoys the protection of the European Convention for the the Protection of Human Rights and Freedoms which the United Kingdom has ratified.

"The present appeal is concerned exclusively with the suspect's right to the privacy of his home... it turns on the respect which Parliament must be understood to pay to the fundamental right of privacy in one's own home which has for centuries been recognised by the common law."

The case in question concerned a police investigation into a road accident where the House of Lords held there was no authority for the police to ask for a breath test in the driver's home when – because they had been asked to leave and had not done so – they were in fact trespassing.

In 1994 another case was heard by Mr Justice Laws at Leicester Crown Court –*Hellewell v Chief Constable of Derbyshire*. This concerned the decision of the Chief Constable to release a police photograph of the plaintiff – who had 19 convictions for theft – to a group of retailers for restricted distribution to their staff in an attempt to reduce shoplifting and harassment. The plaintiff sought an injunction to stop the issuing of the photograph and claimed that in so issuing the photograph the chief constable was guilty of a breach of confidence.

In his judgment, Mr Justice Laws pondered on the legal position concerning the disclosure of photographs in a more general sense, and stated: "I entertain no doubt that the disclosure of a photograph may, in some circumstances, be actionable as a breach of confidence. If someone with a telephoto lens were to take from a distance and with no authority, a picture of another engaged in a private act, this subsequent disclosure of the photograph would, in my judgment, as surely amount to a breach of confidence as if he had found or stolen a letter or diary in which the act was recounted and proceeded to publish it.

"In such a case the law would protect what might reasonably be called a right of privacy, although the name accorded to the cause of action would be a breach of confidence. It is, of course, elementary that, in all cases, a defence based on the public interest would be available."

Public interest

So what would a public interest defence be?

One recent example of photographs taken with a telephoto lens is that of the Duchess of York and a former male friend on holiday. Undoubtedly the photographs were *of* public interest but were they *in* the public interest? This is an argument which is virtually endless and if a plethora of cases were to come to court, each decision would have to be taken on the merits of each case so there can be no hard and fast rule.

Readers will no doubt remember the publication of photographs of Princess Diana which were taken at the gymnasium she used regularly; these were candid shots, taken in a covert manner, of the princess exercising. The Princess settled out of court, although many lawyers believe she would have had no difficulty in establishing a case of breach of confidence. The gymnasium owed her a duty of confidence and the owner would have been one of the defendants if the case had come to court.

On another occasion Princess Diana, the Duchess of York and their children were staying at a holiday villa in the south of France when photographs were taken which were subsequently spread over five pages in the *Daily Mirror*. According to the paper, the pictures were shot from a public place. But it was also reported that the Duchess and the owner of the villa were considering legal action against the newspaper in the French courts for trespass and invasion of privacy.

1996 threw up further incidents involving the Royal Family and in one case even the Queen was involved in potential litigation.

It was reported that the Queen's solicitors in Edinburgh had written on behalf of the Trustees of the Balmoral Estate – the Queen's private home in Scotland – to four freelance photographers requiring them not to enter the grounds of the estate again without permission.

According to a Buckingham Palace spokesman the four had been found on the estate in April 1996 and ignored a request by a police sergeant in the Royal bodyguard to move on. They remained taking photographs of the Royal family for an hour. The spokesman said that if the Queen's request was ignored an injunction – or in Scotland an interdict – would be sought to keep the photographers outside an "exclusion zone". Breaches of such an order can be punished by imprisonment for contempt of court.

Actionable nuisance

The proposition of bringing a breach of privacy action under the heading of actionable nuisance, as suggested by Mr Justice Griffiths in Bernstein's case, is worth further consideration, especially in view of the lengths some professional photographers, and even amateurs, will go to get intimate pictures of personalities relaxing for sale to newspapers and magazines.

Would it be an actionable nuisance if photographer A staked out the house and grounds of a personality from afar, in order to obtain intimate candid photographs with the aid of a telephoto lens?

It has been noted earlier in this chapter that, in certain circumstances, this could constitute a case of aggravated trespass. But for the purpose of an actionable nuisance it is arguable that the answer to the question would be no, for the simple reason that the "victim" of this type of surveillance would be unaware of it and suffer no damage at the time.

On the other hand, if the person concerned knew he or she was under surveillance to such an extent that it rendered it impossible for them to enjoy the use and benefit of their land, it is arguable that a nuisance has been committed as Mr Justice Griffiths suggested. The aggrieved person would then have a remedy in damages and if the nuisance was held to be a bad one, aggravated damages could be awarded if a judge felt this was the right way to mark the court's displeasure at the action of the photographer.

Conspiracy

It is possible to carry this argument forward: if photographer A is sent by a newspaper or magazine to carry out surveillance as described above, and it results in a nuisance being committed on the lines already suggested, are the photographer and publication guilty of conspiracy?

Conspiracy is both a crime and a tort. In this case, as far as the latter is concerned, it involves two or more persons agreeing without lawful justification to cause wilful damage to another or to perform an unlawful act which results in damage. Undoubtedly nuisance is an unlawful act, and consequently in the situation outlined above, both photographer and the publication and/or its directors or employees or both, could be guilty of conspiracy.

The effect of such a finding in a civil court would without doubt mean the award of exemplary damages, heavier than might be usual, which would serve not only to mark the court's disapproval at the conduct of the defendants but also to deter others from acting in a like manner.

However, genuine investigative reporting is protected, as if the purpose of surveillance was to expose crime or iniquity, the person concerned would be unsuccessful in bringing an action, on the grounds that no cause of action follows a base cause.

Confidentiality

Closely allied to privacy is confidentiality. Although there is no legislation as such which codifies the law in this respect, there is a body of case law upon which a claim for breach of confidentiality can easily be based.

What is generally meant by confidentiality as far as the law is concerned, is that a person is entitled to protect his business and trade secrets.

A photographer who is an employer in whatever way is entitled to expect that any information he imparts to his staff, or that they gain during the course of their employment, should remain confidential. This is essential if a photographic studio or picture agency is likely to suffer adversely as a result of an employee revealing information which could lead to financial loss. The same could apply to any branch of the media.

In 1969 Mr Justice Megarry, as he then was, laid down three essential planks on which an action for breach of confidence must be based to be successful.

The first is that information which has been imparted to another person must have the necessary "quality of confidence". This is not difficult to understand; the owner of a studio or picture agency wishes to expand and buy new premises, and confides to existing staff that although willing to pay, say, £30,000 for the lease of new premises, he is only prepared to offer £25,000 in the first instance. If a member of the staff reveals that information to the person with whom his employer is negotiating, and the result is that he has to pay the maximum sum of £30,000, the employee is in breach of confidence.

A similar explanation would suffice to cover the second plank, that the information must have been imparted in circumstances imposing an obligation to keep the information confidential. This point can be underlined by the fact that if the information was gained by an employee during the course of his employment, there is an implied obligation on that employee to keep his employer's business or trade secrets.

The third plank is that there must be unauthorised use of the information to the detriment of the party who communicated it in confidence. Obviously, in the example cited, the detriment would be that the owner of the studio would have no alternative but to pay the full sum of £30,000 when he might have obtained the lease of new premises for less.

Publication of confidential information

News photographers can fall foul of the law of confidentiality if they photograph for the purpose of publication, or even for verification, any document which is the subject of confidence.

One example of this was the case in 1974 of *Distillers v Times Newspapers*, perhaps better known as "the thalidomide case." Distillers was being sued by a number of children who suffered deformities as a result, it was alleged, of their mothers taking the drug thalidomide during pregnancy. During the course of legal proceedings a number of documents of a nature confidential to Distillers were revealed to the legal advisers of the children.

Some of these documents came into the hands of *The Sunday Times*, which was well aware of the source. Distillers argued that, as they were revealed as part of the legal process, the documents were entitled to special protection. The company sought an injunction preventing their use, and were successful.

It is also thought that if Distillers had been unsuccessful in the action for breach of confidence, it would still have had a case for seeking an injunction on the grounds that publication of the documents would be a breach of copyright. Copyright is an important weapon in the armoury of those seeking to enforce confidentiality, especially when breach of confidence involves publication of documents which are subject to copyright.

Note that there is no confidence in iniquity; in other words, if a person receives in conditions of confidentiality, information regarding a proposed breach of the law, there can be no confidential relationship. Thus one of the defences open to a photographer who, during the course of employment or otherwise, photographs documents, is the defence of public interest. In a House of Lords judgment which followed the broadcast of a television programme which used documents confidential to British Steel, Lord Wilberforce referred to circumstances when it would be legitimate to disclose confidential information in the public interest. In his Lordship's view this went beyond iniquity to misconduct generally.

It may also be a breach of confidence if, say, a photograph of a new car prototype, still on the manufacturer's secret list, was published. However, it would have to be that the photographer or publication who obtained the photograph, either from a third party or otherwise, knew that it was confidential.

One way in which the courts can enforce confidentiality is to issue an injunction – usually for just seven days in the first instance as the application is almost certain to be *ex parte*. But the person seeking the injunction will almost certainly have to give an undertaking that if, as a result of the injunction the defendant suffers damage, he will pay those damages and costs if at a later stage it is held that the interim injunction should not have been granted. As in cases of libel, the courts are reluctant to grant injunctions unless it is manifest that the damage done by not granting the injunction would be so great that an award of damages would not be sufficient compensation.

An interesting case was heard in the Chancery Division of the High Court in April 1997. The pop group Oasis had arranged to take photographs for a forthcoming album around the swimming pool of a country club hotel. This involved draining the pool and placing various objects in it as props.

Among fans admitted for the occasion was a freelance photographer for *The Sun*. With others, he took photographs, one of which was similar to the one chosen for the album cover. This picture and others were published in the newspaper the following day, and again a day later with a poster offer to follow.

The plaintiffs applied for an injunction restraining publication until trial of the case – alleging breach of copyright or breach of confidence – could be heard.

Copyright was claimed in the scene itself, in that it was a work of sculpture, collage or artistic craftsmanship. But Mr Justice Lloyd held that the claim was insufficient to grant an injunction on those grounds, or that Noel Gallagher, who supervised the positioning of objects in the pool, held copyright in the unauthorised photograph.

The judge did hold, however, that although photographers among the fans were lawfully at the scene, that did not mean they were free to take photographs; unlike a sketch that could have been drawn from memory, a photograph was a record of the scene organised by the group, and as such was intended to be confidential. He added that it was arguable that if the *Sun* photographer had taken photographs surreptitiously it could be inferred that he knew that photography was not permitted, but had been allowed to remain on that basis.

Mr Justice Lloyd held that a sufficient case of breach of confidence had been made out and granted the injunction until the trial or a further order was made.

Another way – apart from an action for breach of copyright if this should be the correct course of action – to seek compensation for a breach of confidence is an account of profit. The person who is in breach of confidence has to show how much he has made out of the breach, and this will be awarded to the plaintiff in the case.

Such a step was taken by the Princess of Wales after the *Sunday Mirror* and *Daily Mirror* published the gymnasium work-out photographs mentioned earlier. She gained an interim injunction and sued both the owner of the gymnasium and the newspapers. In the out of court settlement the proprietor of the gymnasium agreed to hand over his profits from overseas sales of the pictures. He also agreed that the pictures would not be published again, and not only did he give up all rights in them but handed over the prints and negatives. The Princess also received her legal costs and a sum of money was paid to a charity.

If such an injunction is breached, not only is this likely to increase any damages awarded at a full hearing, it is also likely to result in a fine for contempt of court.

Finally, it must be remembered that if a photographer in the course of his work induces someone to commit a breach of confidence, the photographer – and vicariously his employer if he has one – could be liable in law for damages for inducing the breach.

Crown and Government property

Restrictions also apply to commercial photography in Royal parks and to certain historical monuments and Government offices, all of which come under the authority of the Department of the Environment. Those who wish to photograph in these places have to pay for an annual permit, and any costs incurred by the Department in connection with the photography will also be charged. In certain circumstances the fee can be waived if the photographer is prepared to transfer copyright to the Crown.

It should also be noted that props are not allowed to be used in Royal parks.

No charge is made for news, travelogues, magazine and press facilities, to amateur photographers and media students, or for children's, schools and adult education programmes.

Private property open to the public

Restrictions may or may not be imposed on visitors to private property which is open to the public, such as stately homes or similar buildings such as art galleries or museums. This also applies to places where performances or other events are taking place, such as circuses, concerts, sporting events, etc.

Much depends on the views of the owners of the property or the organisers of the event, although as far as theatres are concerned the question of copyright in the performance or of the set and costume design may also be a factor which has to be considered.

An admission ticket does not give a *carte blanche* to the purchaser; the purchase of a ticket, being given a complimentary ticket, or in the case of some galleries and museums free admission, only implies a licence to enter the premises, and nothing more.

In many of these places notices are prominently displayed stating what the conditions of entry and/or admission are, and these frequently include a ban on photography – particularly "commercial" photography. "Commercial" would cover any sale of photographs for financial gain, even if they were not originally taken with that in mind.

It does not matter for what reason those responsible for imposing the ban have for doing so; it is sufficient that they have the right to do so and they do not have to explain or justify such a ban.

Failure to observe a ban on photography could result in a photographer being treated as a trespasser *ab initio*, for reasons which have been discussed earlier.

It is more likely, however, that when a price for admission has been paid and a person has contravened a ban on photography, that if legal action is taken it would be for breach of contract. This would particularly be the case if photographs taken had been used for a commercial purpose. One of the reasons for bans on photography in some places is to allow the owners and/or organisers to take, or have taken, their own photographs, which they can then use as a commercial asset for promotion and other purposes.

As for theatres and other live performances, a ban on photography is often imposed for a variety of other reasons of which safety, at least in a case of a circus where a flash may well result in injury if it disturbs a performer or an animal, is one. Other reasons are also perfectly sound and would include not knocking performers out of their stride, or disturbing the enjoyment of spectators.

At racecourses, although photography is usually not banned, use of flash equipment is, especially in the paddock and parade ring, as flash is likely to disturb a highly strung thoroughbred racehorse.

Although those responsible for such events can evict photographers who do not observe the rules they cannot and should not attempt to seize either film and/or camera, and only reasonable force can be used to eject the photographer. If undue force is used or film or camera is damaged, the photographer has the right to sue.

Infringement of photographic rights

There is a further possibility in these situations, and that is that exclusive photographic rights to cover a place or event may have been granted to a particular photographer or firm of photographers. Such rights would most usually have been granted for a fee or a share in any sale of photographs.

There is always the possibility that if a photographer who has been granted sole rights – which could be particularly lucrative – becomes aware of unauthorised photography by another, he would seek and in all probability be granted an injunction restraining the other photographer from publishing unauthorised photographs.

Such an action would inevitably be accompanied by an account of and handing over of any profit which may have been made through the unauthorised photography.

10   Injury

All photographers, whether they be amateurs or professionals, will from time to time expose themselves to physical harm for the sake of obtaining a better photograph. Instances when the risk of injury or even death could face a photographer are too numerous to enumerate and, even if they were listed, they would not be exclusive.

In many instances a photographer who takes a risk may do so in a situation where only he is involved, but there are other occasions where third parties are involved and this could cause legal problems and even lead to litigation.

Personal injury

In previous chapters the question of trespass by photographers has been discussed. Now, it is not at all unlikely that a photographer may be trespassing at the time he sustains an injury, but the fact that he is a trespasser does not necessarily preclude him from bringing a claim for damages. Obviously, however, a claim in these circumstances is likely to be strenuously resisted.

Unless a landowner deliberately set out to injure a photographer who was trespassing it is very doubtful that a photographer would recover damages for injuries sustained as a result of a trespass. So one must look primarily at those situations where injury is caused to a photographer who is not a trespasser, since when he is invited into premises or onto land an obligation is placed on the landowner to ensure his safety.

An important, indeed major, piece of legislation in this field is the *Occupiers' Liability Act 1957*. This imposes a common duty of care on all occupiers where lawful visitors to their premises or land are involved. That duty is to take such care as, in all the circumstances, is necessary to ensure the visitor is reasonably safe in using the premises or land for the purpose of which he has been invited to enter or permitted to be there.

Understanding the risks

For the purpose of the photographer who enters premises with consent in pursuit of photographs, the occupier is entitled to assume that the photographer is aware of any risks he may be taking.

For example, a photographer taking photographs of an old building which may have some unsafe features about it, may find himself facing a defence of *volenti non fit injuria* if he sues for injuries sustained. Freely translated, this means that a claim for injury cannot be sustained by a person who knew of a risk and willingly consented to accept it.

Even if the defence of *volenti* is either not raised or is pleaded without success, there is always the possibility that the photographer was guilty of contributory negligence. This would reduce any damages he is entitled to, with the reduction being assessed in accordance with what percentage of fault a judge holds lies with the photographer himself.

As far as those readers who own photographic studios are concerned, potential customers or photographic sundries salesmen have an implied permission to enter. Section 2(1) of the Act referred to above allows an occupier to restrict or exclude his liability but, as photographic studios would be classified as business premises, consideration must be given to the *Unfair Contract Terms Act 1977*. The latter states that the common duty of care in regard to liability for injury or death cannot be excluded.

However, the Act does permit exclusion of liability for damage or other loss on business premises, but only where such an exclusion is reasonable.

Sporting events

The risk of an injury may be most likely at many sporting events, and this is a contentious area. A leading case in this field involved a press photographer who was injured while covering a horse show. This was the case of *Wooldridge v Sumner (1962)*.

In this case the photographer was unfamiliar with horses and had, in fact, ignored the request of a steward to move outside the competition area. The photographer's claim for damages for negligence on the part of the rider was successful in the first instance, but the Court of Appeal reversed the decision.

The court held that negligence had not been established, and Lord Justice Diplock in his judgment laid down certain principles of particular interest to photographers taking pictures at sporting events. "If", he said, "in the course of a game or competition, at a moment when he has not time to think a participant by mistake takes a wrong measure, he is not to be held guilty of negligence."

The learned judge continued: "A person attending a game or competition takes the risk of any damage caused to him by any act of a participant done in the course of and for the purposes of the game or competition, notwithstanding that such an act may involve an error of judgement or a lapse of skill, unless the participant's conduct is such to evince a reckless disregard for the spectator's safety.

"The spectator takes the risk because such an act involves no breach of the duty of care owed by the participant to him. He does not take the risk by virtue of the doctrine expressed or obscured by the maxim *volenti non fit injuria*... the consent that is relevant is not consent to the risk of injury, but consent to the lack of reasonable care that may produce that risk."

Another judgment which underlined that of Lord Justice Diplock was given in the Court of Appeal some nine years later. In this case two spectators sued for injuries sustained at a motor cycle scramble which they were watching from a roped off enclosure. A competitor had left the course and crashed into the enclosure, injuring them.

The Court of Appeal held that the rider had not been negligent, and that it was to have been expected that at such an event loss of control could occur. In its judgment the Court said a competitor must use reasonable care, but this meant reasonable care having regard to the fact that, as a competitor, he was expected to go all out to win and was expected to go as fast as he could, as long as he was not foolhardy.

In these two cases alone it can be seen the risk photographers run of failing in an action for damages should they be injured while photographing sporting events. Nevertheless, every case will depend on its individual circumstances.

Similar considerations would also apply to claims in respect of photographic equipment.

Third party risks

A photographer, like any other citizen, owes a reasonable duty of care to those he is likely to come across during the day by day conduct of his work and life. This, in the case of a photographer, would be in the taking of photographs, but unfortunately it is not possible to state categorically what that care should be.

Each case must, as has been amply demonstrated in previous examples, depend on its own individual merits, but a practical guideline would be to say that a photographer should do nothing that is likely to cause harm to a person or property.

It is particularly advisable that this is remembered when using flash equipment. There are circumstances where the sudden and unexpected use of a flash could lead to a person being injured as a result of unsettling them, or perhaps a horse, whilst engaged in some form of activity. There is little doubt that a court would hold the photographer responsible in law for the subsequent injury.

The employed photographer

In considering liability for injury or death caused as a result of a photographer's actions, there is another important factor to take into consideration – this is whether or not the photographer is an employed person.

If an amateur or self-employed freelance, the photographer is solely liable in damages. But if employed, the employer may well be vicariously liable and both photographer and employer would be joined in any action for damages.

This, of course, can lead to an argument as to what constitutes an employed person, and this may have important repercussions for the freelance photographer who has been given a commission to undertake a specific assignment.

One of the leading legal textbook writers on the subject suggests that a servant – that is, an employed person – can be defined as:

"Any person employed by another to do work for him on terms that he, the servant, is to be subject to the control and direction of his employer in respect of the manner in which the work is to be done as well as the hours to be worked and the remuneration to be paid."

Usually an employer-servant relationship can be determined by the existence of a contract of service which all employees have to receive within thirteen weeks of taking up employment with a particular person or company. Such a contract usually lays down conditions of employment and other relevant matters such as pension, pay, holidays, etc.

On the other hand, a freelance photographer may be more likely to have a contract *for* service with a particular publication. This may be a contract to undertake a specific assignment, or even to be a permanent casual working a specified number of days a week.

It is to be hoped that no publication which has a contract for service with a photographer would hide behind this to seek to avoid vicarious liability. But if this is the case, a court would apply a further test to determine whether a master-servant relationship exists, and this is: who has the right of control over the person carrying out the work?

Originally such a right of control was held to mean the right of an employer to tell his employee how the work was to be done. Today this is unrealistic, especially with competent professional photographers. Consequently this test has been modified and courts now tend to look for who has control over such matters as number of hours to be worked, where they are to be worked, as well as pay etc.

In the case of a freelance photographer doing casual shifts, it would be the right of a newspaper or magazine to select photographic assignments for that person to undertake during the agreed hours of work. Such a contract for service should also include details of payment, expenses to be paid, as well as any other benefits such as pension, holidays or sick pay which may well be the case with what is known as the permanent casual.

Once an employer-employee relationship has been established a photographer who has caused injury should be covered under the *Employers' Liability (Compulsory Insurance) Act 1969* for any injuries or damage to equipment he or colleagues may sustain as a result of negligence or a deliberate act by a photographer.

There is no compulsory cover in respect of injuries to others who are not colleagues, but this is likely to be covered under the employer's public liability policy.

Nevertheless, for peace of mind and financial security, freelance photographers should take out their own public liability insurance and make sure that it covers as many contingencies as possible.

11   Other Restrictions

There are a few further areas where certain prohibitions and restrictions apply, and these will be dealt with in this short chapter.

Nature photography

One field of photography which calls for specialised knowledge, not only of the subject and the art of photography, but of the law as well, is that of nature photography.

This is particularly the case when taking photographs of birds and fledglings at their nests. Although it is not illegal to photograph rare breeding birds, to keep within the law a permit to do so must be obtained if the law contained in the *Wildlife and Countryside Act 1981* is to be observed.

Obviously this restriction only applies to photographers taking very close up photographs of birds in or on their nests, and would not apply if taken from a distance with a telephoto lens so that the birds and fledglings are in no way disturbed.

Previously these licences were issued by the Nature Conservancy Council which covered the whole of the mainland British Isles; today licences are issued by English Nature for England, Scottish National Heritage for Scotland, and the Countryside Council for Wales.

Photographing rare breeding birds without a licence can result in a substantial fine. Basically, all wild birds together with their nests and eggs are protected, with the exception of the following thirteen which are classified as pests. These are:

Collared dove	Crow
Feral pigeon	Great black-backed gull
Herring gull	House sparrow
Jackdaw	Jay
Lesser black-backed gull	Magpie
Rook	Starling
Wood pigeon	

However, obtaining a licence is not just a matter of filling in a form. Quite rightly, the bodies which issue these licences will demand references as to the skill and expertise of applicants before a licence is granted for the first time; thereafter references may not be necessary.

A list of specially protected birds for which a licence is necessary if photographs are to be taken of them on or near the nest, may be obtained from English Nature as detailed in Appendix 2.

Similar restrictions apply to specially protected species of animals, fish and insects, and again a licence must be obtained if they are to be photographed in their place of shelter. A list of these can also be obtained from English Nature.

The laws which protect the countryside and its wildlife also afford special protection to a large number of wild plants. Although it is not necessary to hold a licence to photograph them, it is illegal to pick, uproot or destroy them without a licence or even collect their flowers and seeds. Because photographers, even when using the utmost care and consideration for the environment when photographing wildlife, may inadvertently damage these plants, utmost care must be taken not to break the law.

At the time of writing fines for committing offences under the Act can range from a minimum of £200 to a maximum of £5,000 for offences involving disturbance or damage to those species on the official lists.

English Nature and other bodies have recognised that the photography of wild birds along with other easily visible forms of wildlife has become a widely practised leisure pursuit and have therefore issued special guidelines for photographers. These are summarised in Appendix 2.

Radio controlled equipment

It is illegal to use cameras and accessories which are radio controlled and to do so is an offence under the *Wireless Telegraphy Act 1949*. Under the Act all radio controlled equipment must be licensed, but it is not sufficient just to have a licence; the radio frequencies used have to be approved by the radio regulatory department and this approval is not obtained easily.

One of the reasons for the stringency of the regulations is the fear that in what are, today, extremely crowded airwaves, there may be interference to radio controlled model aircraft, which are also subject to regulations, causing them to go out of control, perhaps resulting in injury or damage. Worse still, there may be interference with radio bands used by emergency services.

It is interesting to note that there appears to be no prohibition on *selling* radio controlled cameras and accessories; the prohibition is on their use without a licence. Photographers should always ask what frequencies are used by radio controlled equipment before buying any such item and then check with the Department of Trade and Industry to ensure the frequency falls into one of those which can be licensed.

The penalties under the Act includes fines and/or a term of imprisonment.

Bye-laws

There are many other places and circumstances where there may be a prohibition on photography; indeed, in some circumstances a ban may be enforced by bye-laws which provide penal sanctions by way of a fine for a breach.

A reference to commercial photography in Royal parks has been made earlier in this book, and there may be other places where similar strictures apply. It is therefore a wise precaution for photographers who may have doubts about whether or not photography is allowed in a certain place, to make sufficient inquiries to ascertain the correct position.

12 Purchase of Equipment

Whether or not photographic equipment is cheap or expensive, the same consumer legislation exists to protect the purchaser. Nowadays protection for the consumer lies in the *Sale of Goods Act 1979*, which replaced an Act of the same title passed back in 1893.

More recently this was amended by the *Sale and Supply of Goods Act 1994*, which clarified and to some extent extended the protection offered under the older Act.

The Sale of Goods Act

Before examining those parts of the Act which are most likely to affect the photographer, it must be remembered that any purchase is a contract.

A simple contract, yes, but a contract nevertheless. It means that the seller offers goods at a certain price to a potential buyer who can make up his own mind as to whether or not he wishes to buy at the price quoted. If he does, then a binding contract is entered into between buyer and seller, and is equally binding whether it is oral (spoken) or written. Quite obviously, the purchaser of photographic equipment is most likely to enter into an oral contract which is effectively sealed when the purchase price (or part of it if the equipment is purchased on hire purchase, by credit sale agreement or leased) is paid.

As far as the purchaser of photographic equipment is concerned, he can first look to Section 14(2) of the 1979 Act for protection. This section reads:

"Where the seller sells goods in the course of a business there is an implied condition that the goods supplied under the contract are of merchantable quality, except that there is no condition (a) as regards defects specifically drawn to the buyer's attention before the contract is made, or (b) if the buyer examines the goods before the contract is made, as regards defects which that examination ought to reveal."

Section 14(6) of the Act states:

"Goods of any kind are of merchantable quality... if they are fit for the purpose or purposes for which goods of that kind are commonly bought as it is reasonable to expect having regard to any description applied to them, the price (if relevant) and all other relevant circumstances."

The *Sale and Supply of Goods Act 1994* substituted the term "satisfactory quality" for "merchantable quality" and extended the definition of "fitness for purpose" to "fitness for all intended purposes". This now covers such aspects as freedom from even minor defects, appearance, safety and durability.

It is worth noting that Section 61(1) of the 1987 Act says that the word "quality" in relation to goods includes their state or condition. This means that a photographer who buys a camera or any piece of equipment is entitled to expect it to be reasonably fit for its normal purpose and free from defects.

However a photographer who accepts equipment having had a defect pointed out to him, or having been given a chance to inspect the equipment, has no comeback under the Act as he is deemed to have accepted the article when he was aware, or should have been aware and would have been so if he had inspected the equipment, of the defect.

On the other hand the buyer of a camera or accessory which is defective in its actual mechanism – which could not be seen without taking it apart – has a piece of equipment which is definitely not of satisfactory quality. Consequently the purchaser does have a comeback against the dealer.

Equipment must also be fit for the purpose for which it was bought, if the particular reason for which the equipment is required is made known to the seller. So a photographer who asks for a camera or accessory with the capacity to do certain tasks – such as high-speed sports photography – and is sold one which does not meet the requirements, can demand his money back. Such a demand must be made as soon as is reasonably possible after a defect is discovered or the buyer realises he has not got what he wanted. Bear in mind, however, that the idea of satisfactory quality and fitness for purpose may often depend upon what is considered customary use for a particular piece of equipment.

The two conditions – satisfactory quality and fitness for purpose – are what the law calls "implied terms" in all sales.

There is also a third term which is contained in Section 13 of the Act. This is that goods must fit their description, which must be described either orally by a salesman, or in writing on a package, in a mail order catalogue or in an advertisement.

The *Trade Descriptions Act 1968* makes it a criminal offence for a trader to misrepresent goods or a services. Any complaint has to be made to local trading standards officers, who have the discretion to prosecute or not. If a prosecution is decided upon, it does not follow that the disgruntled purchaser will automatically get a refund of money paid. Although courts do have the power to order a convicted trader to make restitution, not all courts do so. However, a conviction under the Act is certainly almost all that is necessary to establish a claim in a civil court.

Rights of the purchaser

As noted above, the three implied terms of any sale contained in the Act are that the goods should fit their description, be of satisfactory quality, and be fit for their purpose. If the goods fail to measure up to any of these three criteria the consumer is entitled to a full refund; he is not obliged to accept a replacement or repair.

There are circumstances where defective goods can be kept and just part of the purchase price refunded, the sum paid being the difference between the value of the goods without the defect and the value with the defect. In Scotland, where the law is different, it is more than probable that a replacement can be insisted upon.

Do not be fobbed off with a credit note offered by a shop; in law a customer who has purchased a defective item or items which are not satisfactory or fit for the purpose is entitled to a monetary refund and not a credit note. Obviously it is in the interest of the shop to offer a credit note as it means that the customer will have to purchase further goods from that particular shop, but this is far from the intention of the legislation.

The same applies to guarantees. They are useful as they give the consumer the knowledge that if, during the period of the guarantee repairs are necessary, those repairs will be carried out by skilled craftsmen using proper materials and component parts.

But if equipment proves to be seriously defective within a short time of purchase, it must be remembered that a contract exists between consumer and seller, not consumer and manufacturer. Legally the manufacturer is not a party to the contract – unless the consumer is able to bring a case under the provisions of the product safety regulations contained in the *Consumer Protection Act 1987* and the *General Products Safety Regulations 1994*. But it is submitted that it is very unlikely that the bulk of photographic equipment would cause injury if properly handled.

So if a camera or accessory proves to be seriously defective the proper channel for the purchaser to follow is to seek to enforce his rights against the seller; the dealer has his own rights against the manufacturer which he can enforce if he so wishes.

In the event that the dealer with whom the consumer entered into a contract to purchase equipment has gone out of business, it is likely that the manufacturer would honour the contract.

Consequential loss

If a piece of defective equipment results in what is termed consequential loss or damage, which may fairly and reasonably be considered as rising from the defect, the consumer has the right to an additional claim for damages.

However, the right to claim for consequential loss or damage is restricted, in as much as a complainant must prove that such loss or damage could be within the contemplation of the dealer when the defective equipment was sold.

This is necessarily restrictive, otherwise every seller could be at risk of a damage claim following the sale of a particular item. To give an example: if a flashgun was so seriously defective as to explode injuring the user, it could be submitted that this is something the dealer could reasonably contemplate happening if the explosion was due to an integral defect of which the dealer knew.

In such circumstances the photographer could bring an action against the dealer, or the manufacturer under the product safety regulations, not only for breach of implied terms that the flashgun was of satisfactory quality but also for the consequential damage it caused. It is more probable in those circumstances that the dealer himself might join against the manufacturer in the action or, at a later date, make a claim against them.

Exclusion clauses

From time to time written contracts of sale or guarantees contain an exclusion or exemption clause which is a notice which purports to deny the consumer some of his rights as far as the trader is concerned. Such clauses may take many forms; some may disclaim any responsibility for any loss or damage, although this will more generally apply to services rather than goods.

Other exclusion or exemption clauses may seek to substitute statutory rights in favour of rights which are more favourable to the dealer or supplier than to the consumer. However, today all reputable manufacturers state that accepting the terms and conditions of a guarantee in no way precludes the consumer from exercising his statutory rights.

Even though reputable dealers do not indulge in "bad practices" as far as the consumer is concerned, the consumer is further protected by the stringent conditions of the *Supply of Goods (Implied Terms) Act 1973* and the *Unfair Contract Terms Act 1977*. Furthermore, any guarantee which omits the declaration about a consumer's statutory rights would be in breach of the *Consumer Transactions (Restrictions on Statements) Order 1976* and *Amendment Order 1978*.

As a result, no guarantee or contract for sale can exclude basic liability under the *Sale of Goods Act*, or liability for negligence causing injury or death. Furthermore if a trader seeks to exclude liability under the *Misrepresentation Act 1967* (for England and Wales) or the *Misrepresentation Act (Northern Ireland) 1967*, the trader would have to prove that such exclusions were reasonable in all the circumstances. This can be extremely difficult to do.

In all transactions where there are exemption or exclusion clauses, the test the courts apply is one of "reasonableness", and the onus is on the person seeking to avoid liability to prove that such a clause was reasonable.

To succeed in doing so, the person seeking to enforce the exclusion clause must prove it was fair and reasonable in the circumstances of the particular transaction, the circumstances of which were, or ought to have been, reasonably known to, or likely to be considered by, both parties to the contract.

One of the main items a court will look at is the bargaining power and position of both parties. If a trader who is seeking to enforce the exemption clause is in a stronger position than his customer – which could well be the case if the particular goods and/or services he provided could not be obtained without travelling some distance – he is not likely to be able to seek refuge in the clause.

It is worth stressing that on the whole those who deal in cameras and photographic accessories are reputable. Unfortunately not all assistants who work in shops are as fully aware of consumer rights as their employers. In such circumstances, the employer is liable. However, ignorance on the part of an assistant may be a mitigating factor as far as an offence of a criminal nature is concerned (most likely under the *Trade Descriptions Act*), though not in any claim for damages.

Misrepresentation

The *Misrepresentation Act 1967* is the usual vehicle by which a purchaser can sue a seller who is a private individual rather than a full time trader. But it can also be used in a dispute with a trader if ignorance on the part of an assistant leads to a misrepresentation being made about a camera or an accessory. Such misleading statements are covered by the above Act.

This particular Act does not apply to Scotland, although the law there is very similar.

There are three form of misrepresentation: innocent, negligent and fraudulent. If the statement is a term of the contract, the buyer will be entitled to damages even if the statement is made innocently. Otherwise, if not a term of the contract, damages will only be awarded if the statement was made negligently or fraudulently.

Basically, such a statement is something said by or on behalf of the seller which induces the purchaser to buy.

An innocent misrepresentation occurs when a seller makes a statement about goods which he believes to be true at the time, as a result of which a purchase follows. What is taken into account when deciding whether or not a statement resulted in a would-be buyer purchasing a particular item, is the strength of the statement, the importance attached to it by the buyer, and the relative degree of knowledge of both seller and buyer. Of course, in a store specialising in photographic equipment, in all probability the proprietor and/or his assistants will have greater knowledge than a potential buyer.

Innocent misrepresentation occurs when the seller makes a statement about the goods which he believes to be true, but when a seller makes a statement about the goods which he has no reasonable grounds to believe to be true, he is then guilty of negligent misrepresentation. This entitles the purchaser to compensation in England and Wales, where it is only necessary to prove that such a misrepresentation was made. In Scotland it is necessary to prove not only that a misrepresentation was made, but that it was made negligently, and this is a higher standard of proof than is required in England and Wales.

Fraudulent misrepresentation means that a deliberately untrue statement has been made. This would be the case if a salesman lied about the capability of a camera to do certain jobs and as a result of such statements the would-be purchaser buys the camera. Compensation for such a fraudulent misrepresentation can be obtained, if it is too late to rescind the contract.

Furthermore, if, as a result of that misrepresentation, the photographer incurred expenses in seeking to take photographs which were beyond the technical capacity of the camera, he would be entitled to claim damages for any loss suffered as a result of his reliance on the fraudulent statement.

It has to be remembered that for a disgruntled consumer to rely on the *Misrepresentation Act*, the misrepresentation must refer to the past or present and not the future. Thus in the example quoted above, if the salesman said he had used a particular camera for such and such a purchase with satisfactory results and this was not so, this would be sufficient to prove misrepresentation.

On the other hand, if he said he believed or was of the opinion that the camera was capable of producing certain types of photography, there would be no misrepresentation, because not only would such a claim refer to the future but it would also be a statement of opinion.

This only underlines the fact that to succeed in a claim in which misrepresentation is alleged, the misrepresentation must refer to a question of fact, or of law, if it is to be successful.

Hire purchase and credit sales

Many photographers buy more expensive items of equipment on hire purchase, a legally binding agreement under which the goods are hired to the buyer with an option to buy at the end of the hire period for a nominal sum. During this period the goods involved cannot be sold or disposed off without the consent of the seller.

Providing a minimum amount has been paid, the goods cannot be repossessed without a court order if the hirer defaults on his monthly payments.

With a credit sale, however, the goods become the property of the purchaser immediately. A major piece of legislation controlling sales in which credit is involved is the *Consumer Credit Act 1974*, which extends the protection afforded by the *Hire Purchase Act 1965*. If the amount of credit involved is between £50 and £15,000 the purchaser must receive a copy of the agreement, which must state the rate of interest charged. Note that the sums of £50 to £15,000 refer not to the value of the goods, but to the credit granted.

Many purchases are now made by credit cards, which are also controlled by the *Consumer Credit Act*. But whatever the form of credit, it in no way takes away the rights of a consumer under the *Sale of Goods Act*.

Having been granted credit – which today is usually after a check with a credit agency – there is a legal obligation on the borrower to honour the contract and make repayments whenever they are due. Dependent upon the amount of the debt outstanding, goods can only be repossessed with a court order.

In today's economic climate those who grant credit are usually sympathetic to a borrower who falls upon hard times provided that changed circumstances are made known to the lender as soon as possible. In most cases of genuine hardship, lenders are willing to reduce the amount of monthly payments or accept an interest-only payment leaving the balance to be paid off when the borrower is in a better financial position. Again a condition would be that any change in the financial circumstances of the borrower or hirer is made know to the appropriate source of finance immediately.

13 Photographic Services

Exclusion clauses have been considered in the previous chapter as far as the purchase of equipment is concerned, but it is now necessary to look at them in relation to photographic services, the most notable two circumstances being developing and/or printing, and equipment repairs.

Today nothing poses more difficulties for photographers than the services they receive or, perhaps to be more accurate, do not receive from the numerous firms offering developing and printing services. The problem of lost or damaged films seems to be one that affects almost every serious photographer at some time.

One of the most contentious issues concerns the exemption or exclusion clauses which most processing firms fall back on when problems arise.

Exclusion clauses in D&P

In most cases such an exemption clause is likely to be expressed in the following terms:

"Whilst every care is taken of film(s), prints and negatives our responsibility for lost or damaged film is limited to the cost of the unexposed film and the processing charge."

Sometimes the exclusion clause may contain the expression "even if our fault", but the result remains the same. This type of exclusion clause was challenged some years ago by a photographer who submitted to a D&P firm a roll of film he had taken of a friend's wedding. It was his intention to present them in an album as a wedding present. In the event the film was damaged and the photographer brought a case against the D&P firm.

The case was first heard using the arbitration method then available in county courts for small claims, and the photographer was awarded £75 compensation. The firm then appealed to Exeter County Court, where Judge Clarke upheld the arbitration findings and award of £75.

As has been previously discussed, the *Unfair Contracts Term Act 1977* laid down that exclusion or exemption clauses would only be upheld by the courts if they were fair and reasonable in all the circumstances. In the Exeter case, Judge Clarke clearly found that the clause was unfair and unreasonable. But while this was a step forward, it did not create a precedent. Because it was a county court and not a High Court decision, the precedent is not binding, and consequently another judge might take a different view if the occasion arose again.

In December 1996, *The Times* reported that a scientist had claimed in Leeds County Court that Boots should pay him £30,000 for an expedition to the Arctic Circle so that he could retake pictures lost by Boots after he lodged a film to be developed with the company.

According to the scientist the 36 photographs he took at Franz Joseph Land, which is only 70 miles from the North Pole, were essential for research he was doing on climatic changes. Boots, he claimed, should pay the cost of an expedition back to the Pole to reshoot the pictures. Apparently the particular branch of Boots with which the film was lodged had a problem in developing it and sent it to their specialist laboratory – without getting the consent of the scientist – and the film was lost in transit.

The court was told that Boots – who were not represented at the hearing – at first denied responsibility for the loss but now admitted liability. The case was adjourned, and at the time of going to press with this book there had been no further developments on the legal front.

However, partly as a result of the case, the Photo Marketing Association – of which Boots is a member – met to discuss the problem of disclaimers of liability. This also followed reports that PMA members were being ordered by the Office of Fair Trading to remove disclaimer notices from their premises which, the OFT claimed, were illegal and unfair to customers.

In April of 1997 a meeting between representatives of the PMA and the OFT was held to discuss what a member of the association described as not a disclaimer, but a statement outlining the action a processor would take should something go wrong, and which most people would accept as being fair and reasonable. It was hoped that the OFT would consider this statement to be one that could be properly displayed by all processors.

The most usual form of exclusion clause encountered is likely be before a film is accepted for processing or equipment for repair.

This may well take the form of a statement saying that no liability for loss or damage will be accepted, or there could be a variation and/or a further statement seeking to limit the amount of compensation which will be paid unless an additional sum is paid by way of insurance. In many circumstances this could be construed as fair and reasonable, and this would be the case if the consumer could find a similar service in the same area where such clauses were not applied. If, however, similar services could not be found within a reasonable distance, it is likely a court would find the exclusion clause to be unfair and unreasonable in all the circumstances.

Similarly with regard to the bargaining power of the service supplier. If he is in a much stronger position than the consumer and able to dictate his own terms, this could be construed as being unfair and unreasonable in certain circumstances.

Many major firms offer developing and printing services by post and the advertisements for such services very often take the form of an envelope inserted in a magazine or newspaper, or even on a stand at places where the public gather in large numbers.

Details of the offer and price are printed on the envelope and often may include a clause disclaiming or limiting liability. These clauses may or may not be considered fair and reasonable; much would depend on the size of the printed conditions. If the print is so small that it is difficult for the average person to read it, then it is likely that such a clause will be considered invalid on the grounds that it could not be read by users of the service without mechanical aids to sight.

The Supply of Goods and Services Act

The *Supply of Goods and Services Act 1982* filled a gap which was not provided by the *Sale of Goods Act 1979*. The latter, as was seen in the previous chapter, provided protection for purchasers of goods but not of services. For our purposes it is only necessary to consider services, as the "goods" part of the title refers here not to goods purchased but to those gained by the collection of coupons or tokens.

Among the provisions of the Act are three which are of importance not only to photographers as users of photographic services, but as users of any other service. These provisions are that the service provided – and this would certainly include developing and printing as well as repairs to equipment – should be carried out with a reasonable standard of care, within a reasonable time, and with a reasonable charge.

This is an important piece of consumer legislation because it codifies what can be expected legally from those who provide services. Unfortunately claims under the Act are likely to be small and dealt with by small claims courts or county courts whose judgments are not binding as are those of the High Court.

It will be seen that the touchstone of this particular portion of the legislation is the word "reasonable", to which must be added: "in the circumstances of a particular case."

It is arguable that a photographer who uses the services of a D&P firm which offers to process and print a roll of film for, say, £2.99 in one hour, may not be expected to receive the same standard of reasonable care as a firm which offers the same service for a greater sum and under the banner of "professional" processing. But as most developing of colour film today is done mechanically, a better example for our purposes would be repairs and/or servicing of equipment.

Standards of care

For reputable photographic dealers who offer a repair and servicing service, there is no doubt that standard of reasonable care would be held to be what a trained and competent service engineer, properly supervised, should be expected to bring to a particular task. Failure to show that standard of care and skill could lead to a claim for damages if the repair or service is not carried out in a proper and reasonable manner.

There is no doubt that a photographer could recover the basic costs of the repair, but the next question to be asked is: What damage flows from the failure to exercise suitable care and skill?

If the answer to this is that the equipment was rendered virtually unworkable there is little doubt that a claim for the cost of replacement would be easily quantifiable and successful. However, if the photographer was a professional and lost a lucrative assignment through failure of the equipment or, as could be equally valid, an amateur photographer travelled to the Himalayas at great expense especially to take photographs, undoubtedly both would have a claim for additional damages. The professional for loss of profit from his commissioned job and any other incidental expenses involved before the faulty repair work was discovered. Equally the amateur for expenses incurred and even, perhaps, an award of damages for the disappointment factor.

But the crucial question is, could and should the person carrying out the repair or service reasonably be expected to know of the intentions of the photographers outlined in the above paragraph? Quite probably not, unless the professional was known to the dealer carrying out the repair and that dealer should have been well aware that the equipment was used for professional purposes.

So, although it may seem an unnecessary and extremely pedantic step, a photographer seeking to have work done to his camera before setting out to capture on film some specific place or event which involves considerable expense and/or a fee, should make this fact known to the engineer or his employer. They are then on notice that failure to carry out the repair or service in a proper or satisfactory manner could lead to the photographer being out of pocket. They should equally be aware that such a failure could result in financial loss to the photographer for which they (the repairers) would be held responsible.

Time

Similar considerations apply to the work being carried out within a reasonable time, unless the contrary is agreed. Again, the yardstick is what would be considered to be a "reasonable" period of time.

Undoubtedly the skill and competence of those offering the service would be considered, as would the time of year if it is known that certain times are busier than others. Perhaps the most important factor to be considered is the complexity of a repair and the ability to get new parts if they are required within a short time. If an estimate is given of how long the work will take – with the caveat that if a part or parts are needed it may be longer – it is up to the photographer to decide whether he wishes to leave his equipment with that repairer or not.

However, if the photographer tells a repairer that it is essential that the work be carried out within a certain time and the repairer agrees to do this without any caveat as to the possibility of delay if parts are needed, then a contract has been entered into of which time is the essence. Failure to carry out the repair within the specified time is a breach from which damages can flow if the repairer could reasonably be expected to know that, apart from inconvenience to the photographer, there would also be pecuniary loss.

Charges

Finally there is the question of what is a reasonable charge.

In the event of a dispute, the repairer would have to prove that his charge was reasonable in all the circumstances. This would involve not only whether or not the rate was consistent with that charged by others in the area, but that if parts were needed they were within the manufacturer's price guide range.

A final factor to be considered is the reasonableness or otherwise of charges for overheads and the profit factor. Of course, if a price is agreed upon at the outset the photographer can refuse to pay more if the repairer has underestimated the length of the job, or the cost of parts, because a contract has been entered into at an agreed price.

Assessing damages

There is a great difference between establishing liability and gaining an award of damages in respect of a damaged or lost film. To understand why, it is necessary to understand that the concept of an award of damages is not for the enrichment of a victim of negligence or breach of contract, but to put them back into the position they would have been in had there been no negligence or contractual breach.

Consequently, it has to be asked how can damages be quantified for a particular lost or damaged roll of film? As has been referred to earlier in this chapter, it is much easier to quantify damages for a professional photographer for whom loss or damage to films will inevitably lead to a loss of fees. But for other photographers a different criterion for assessing loss must be applied.

Many of the complaints which follow a film lost or damaged during the development process refer to pictorial records of holidays or a special family event. A judge or arbitrator dealing with a claim for damages for loss of or damage to films of special personal value has to ask the question: Did the negligence spoil the occasion?

Common sense dictates that the answer must be no, because, at the time of the holiday or family celebration, the question of the future negligence of the D&P firm did not arise. Such negligence was a *post facto* occurrence which, by no conceivable stretch of the imagination, could be held to have spoiled the event itself.

On the other hand, a photographer who sets out on a specific photographic mission with, say, the sole intention of capturing on film the Pyramids or the Taj Mahal, could have a claim. The strength of such a claim would depend on one main factor: could the processing firm have reasonably foreseen the loss which would follow from negligence?

The answer must again be no; any firm which receives film either through the post or over the counter, directly at its own premises or through an agent, is in no position to know whether a roll of film depicts a subject for which the photographer has gone to considerable expense, or just snapshots taken in his own back garden.

If the films are handed to a processing firm at its own premises, one way to protect oneself against financial loss is to declare that the photographs are of special value and explain why. Even then it may be necessary for the photographer to take out insurance to cover against financial loss in the event of damage.

Taking precautions

In circumstances such as those above it is best to put in writing why the films have a particular value to the photographer. This will put the D&P firm on notice that there was a high cost in getting the photographs.

If the photographs have been commissioned, the value of the commission should be declared together with any expenses incurred. Otherwise any claim for loss of earnings would be met by the perfectly reasonable defence that the firm was unable to reasonably foresee that there was commercial value in the film.

Many firms offering developing and printing services now display in a prominent position a warning that if a film to be processed has a value over and above the nominal sum usually paid if anything goes wrong, this should be made known at the time it is handed in. In most cases a small additional charge will be made, as a form of insurance premium for increased cover.

Although many consider this a step in the right direction, the onus still remains on the photographer to take this step and accept the extra cost, when the onus really should be on the developer to ensure that his customer does not suffer as a result of negligence.

This uncertainty over what recompense, if any, a photographer may expect to receive for films lost or damaged, causes great concern to serious amateurs and professional photographers who may have invested large sums of money to obtain the photographs.

It is arguable that developing and printing firms should always carry sufficient insurance to meet genuine claims, but this still does not appear to be the position today. So photographers should always ask if insurance cover is available, and favour those firms that offer cover as a standard feature.

It could be that if a precedent was set by a decision in either the Queen's Bench Division of the High Court, the Court of Appeal, or even the House of Lords, which placed responsibility of making full recompense for all forms of loss which followed negligence on the part of a processing firm, steps to take out such insurance would soon follow.

Insurance

Until then, the photographer who wishes to protect his investment in time and expense in taking photographs must insure them himself.

From time to time there are complaints from those heavily involved in the photographic field that it is difficult to obtain a policy to cover all eventualities. This may well be the case with ordinary insurance companies, but there are today a number of specialist companies that have policies tailored for photographers according to their needs. There are also many syndicates of underwriters at Lloyd's of London who will take all types of risks including those involved in the photographic field.

Photographers seeking to cover themselves should contact a specialist company or reputable broker and present them with written details of the type of policy that is required, either for a period of a year or perhaps just for a specific length of time to cover a particular assignment.

So that a true premium reflecting the risk the insurer has to carry is reached, It will also be necessary for the insured to declare an accurate as possible estimate of costs involved in obtaining certain photographs and, if it is a commissioned assignment, the fee to be paid. As in all cases of insurance, which will be dealt with further in Chapter 15, full disclosure is essential.

European law

In recent years European Union legislation, especially in the field of consumer protection and regulation, has been introduced into the law of this country. This is perhaps an appropriate point to take a brief look at recent enactments which have impinged on or strengthened consumer law in the UK.

Under the *Unfair Terms in Consumer Contracts Regulations 1994*, as far as consumer contracts are concerned, there is the definition of an unfair term as one which: "..contrary to the requirement of good faith causes a significant imbalance in the parties' rights and obligations under the contract to the detriment of the consumer."

If "good faith" becomes an important part of any dispute it is laid down that in assessing whether or not there has been good faith, the following factors shall be taken into consideration:

The strength of the bargaining position of the parties to a contract;
Whether or not the consumer was induced to agree to the term in dispute;
Whether the goods or services provided were sold or supplied against a special order of the consumer;
The extent to which the supplier or seller had dealt fairly and with equity with the consumer.

Another set of regulations, the *General Products Safety Regulations 1994*, to a certain extent amended the *Consumer Protection Act*

1987, which has already been referred to. The general safety requirement under that Act covered a broad spectrum of supplying goods. Now under the regulations a general safety requirement must be complied with if products are to be placed on the market by either producers or distributors.

The term "producers" covers manufacturers – but only those who are established within the European Community – who assemble products and put their name or trade mark on the product.

For manufacturers outside the Community – which would, of course, cover the many makers of cameras and photographic equipment based in the Far East – responsibility devolves on either their representatives or, if there is no established representation within the Community, the importer.

As far as these particular regulations are concerned, the products covered are more extensive than those under the 1987 Act. Anything intended for consumers, or likely to be used by them and supplied during the course of a commercial transaction, is caught by the regulations even if it is used or reconditioned items.

Many of the new regulations referred to above are, like much legislation, expressed in complex legal language. As always it cannot be stressed too strongly that in cases which may be complicated it is essential to seek legal advice; in only the most simple and straightforward of cases should any layman attempt to act for himself.

Finally, local trading standards offices have a series of useful leaflets which explain in everyday language the rights of consumers, while similar help and advice can be obtained from Citizens Advice Bureaux.

14 Business Matters

To run one's own business is a laudable ambition, especially in the case of a photographer who is in the happy position of being able to make a living from what may have started out as – and probably still is – his hobby.

However, it is not as simple as that; having taken the decision to make a living from any activity it is vitally important that a key question is asked and answered at the outset if the business is not to be a disaster. That question is: what type of business is this to be?

Starting a business

If a photographer has a nose for news and a flair for taking newsworthy and dramatic photographs, he can establish himself as a freelance news and current affairs photographer with very little difficulty. However, the person most likely to succeed in what can be a precarious business is most likely to be a former staff photographer for a newspaper, magazine or news gathering organisation. And before rushing into a business of this type the photographer should be aware that he may well run into the type of contractual difficulties with copyright that are referred to in Chapter 3 of this book.

Others may be in the business of producing pictures and features for magazines and picture agencies, or perhaps doing small location assignments for local clients.

For these types of work, the photographer basically needs nothing more apart from the ability to take and sell his photographs as well as the knowledge of how to operate within the legal requirements outlined earlier in this book. But of course it is not quite as simple as that. Not only are a telephone, answering machine and even a mobile phone necessary requirements, so too is a motor vehicle.

And for all these it is important that there is ample insurance cover, especially as far as the vehicle is concerned. Not only must it be insured for business use but it is also essential that the cover also includes theft of equipment from the vehicle – something which is not always automatically covered in a standard car insurance policy.

So starting a business is not always as simple as first appears.

A photographer who sets up in business under a name other than his own does not have to register the business name as in the past, but he must be careful not to use a name which is either nationally known or known in the locality in which his business is operating. If he does there is a possibility of a passing off action.

However, if a business name is used there is a legal requirement for any letterheads, bills, receipts, etc, to carry the name and permanent address of where the business is run from and where all correspondence in connection with the business can be sent.

There are three basic types of business a photographer could establish: a one man business, a partnership, or a limited company. The simplest of these is the one man or sole trader business but this can have disadvantages, the main one being if it is necessary to raise finance to provide premises and/or equipment.

Finance

Many one man businesses start with little capital and indeed, a photographer who has his own equipment has initially little need of capital provided he is assured of sufficient work to bring in money to cover his basic needs. The problem arises should the business seek further capital for either expansion or to tide it over a slack period.

The obvious place from which to raise capital is the photographer's own bank, which will certainly require security of some form. If the loan is large then the security may well be in the form of the photographer giving the bank a charge over the photographer's house. But the bank loan most certainly would only be equal to the value of the house after a mortgage has been paid off and the current outstanding amount owed on such a mortgage.

This poses two problems; the first is that the terms of any mortgage may well include the need for the building society or other financial institution which has granted the mortgage to give its permission for a second mortgage or charge to be placed on the property.

Whether or not this permission is necessary, the lender will require not only the owner or joint owner to consent to the house being pledged as a security, but any other person who has an interest in the equity of the house will also have to consent. In most cases this will be the photographer's spouse or partner if he or she are not already joint owners. In certain circumstances it is conceivable that it could include a relative if that relative had paid a share of either the mortgage or the upkeep of the house.

There is a major drawback to running a one man business and that is the risk of the owner being forced into bankruptcy if the business fails. Even if the photographer's house has not been pledged as security against a loan, in the last resort creditors can get a court order for the house to be seized and sold to pay off outstanding debts.

Partnerships

The *Partnership Act 1890* describes a partnership as a relationship which exists between persons – obviously, two or more – carrying on a business in common with a view to profit. If two photographers get together to carry on business, perhaps as a photographic news agency or to open a commercial studio, unless there is something in writing to suggest otherwise, the law would undoubtedly consider this to be a partnership.

Similarly, unless there is agreement to the contrary – and if so, preferably in writing – the Act states that all profits must be shared equally, as must losses. Under the Act, individual partners have the right to be paid by other partners for individual payments made, or liabilities incurred, in the course of running the business.

It is quite possible that an experienced photographer who has created a flourishing business over the years may wish to take a younger person into partnership. If this is the case and the new partner is not to receive half the profits, it will be necessary for a partnership agreement to be drawn up which states in what proportion the profits – and losses if they are incurred – are to be divided, and who will have the major say in any decisions which may affect the day-to-day or future running of the business.

Such matters as payment of any pension when one partner retires, or whether other persons can be taken into the partnership, should also be included in the agreement. At this stage a word of warning must be sounded; photographers, or anyone else for that matter, going into partnership should never attempt to draw up a partnership agreement on their own.

Entering into a partnership is a matter of such importance that the advice of a solicitor should always be sought, especially when drawing up a partnership agreement. It is essential that all parties to such an agreement are fully aware of each other's responsibilities, rights and share of any losses or profits.

It must also be kept in mind that partners have a collective responsibility not only for running the business but for any debts incurred. Creditors are entitled to proceed against the partner who is financially best able to meet their legitimate claims.

Usually a partner will not be held responsible for debts incurred before he joined the partnership nor for those after he has ceased to be a partner. Naturally he will be liable with other partners for debts incurred when he was a member of the partnership.

Most partnerships are created for an unlimited period of time, but this does not mean that a partner cannot be ousted if there is a genuine reason for the other partner(s) to want him to leave.

There can be written into partnership agreements conditions under which a partner can be removed and, in extreme cases, a court can order the dissolution of a partnership. It cannot be stressed strongly enough that there is a need for obtaining legal advice before even the simplest of partnership agreements are entered into.

Companies

The third way of running a business is by creating a limited company which then has a separate legal entity and is responsible for its own debts.

Shareholders are legally liable only to the extent of the shares they hold. Thus if two photographers form a limited company with a capital of £5,000 with each having 2,500 £1 shares for which they have paid the full price, and the company goes into liquidation (companies go into liquidation; only individuals go bankrupt) they have lost their original investment and nothing more.

On the other hand, if either or both subscribers to the company have taken out 2,500 shares but have only paid, say, 50p a share, they will be liable in the event of the company being wound up to pay the balance of the money owed on the shares they hold to meet the demands of any creditors.

A company must either be a private one or a public limited company (PLC), but for the purpose of this book it will be assumed that the photographer wishing to form a company is thinking in terms of a private one. Indeed a public limited company has to have a minimum capital of £50,000 and can have its shares available to the public through the Alternative Investment Market, or a full quotation – after meeting stringent conditions – on the Stock Exchange.

Legal requirements of companies

There are a number of important but not particularly onerous legal formalities which have to be gone through before a company can be formed, and it is worth seeking the advice of either a solicitor or an accountant.

The formalities consist of lodging a number of documents with the Registrar of Companies which, for a private company, number no more than four. These are:

The Memorandum of Association;
The Articles of Association;
A statement of the authorised share capital;
A statutory declaration that all the requirements of the various Companies Acts have been met.

Although all of the above are necessary, perhaps the two most important are the Memorandum of Association and the Articles of Association. The Memorandum contains the name of the company and states whether the registered office – which need not be the place from where the business is run and in the case of small companies is often that of the company's accountant – is situated in

England and Wales or Scotland.

The Memorandum must also contain the objects of the company and it is advisable for these objects to be drawn as widely as possible. For the photographer setting up a company, wisdom dictates that he should include in the Memorandum of Association the rights of the company to undertake any ancillary business associated with photography or its offshoots, for example the selling and processing of films, or photographic equipment and accessories.

The reason for drawing the objects as widely as possible is to enable the company to branch out into fields covered by the objects which, at the time of inception might not have been thought possible. Unless these potential future objectives are stated in the Memorandum of Association, they can be held to be *ultra vires* and as such unlawful. Of course it is possible to change the Memorandum of Association at a later date but this can be costly.

This Memorandum will also state the amount of share capital, and that the liability of members (shareholders) is limited.

The difference between the Memorandum and the Articles of Association is that the latter is what may be termed a domestic document, inasmuch as it determines how shares are to be transferred, the rights of shareholders, how directors are to be appointed and removed, when meetings are held and, perhaps more important, the borrowing powers of the company.

Unless the company has the power to borrow money it is prohibited by law from doing so. Even if the company has borrowing powers, a financial institution will take a commercial view of a request for finance. If the company's assets are considered to be insufficient to cover the amount of the loan, other security will be required and this could well be a charge on property owned by directors. If the only tangible asset owned by a director is the director's own house, the same considerations apply as far as any other person with an interest in the equity of the house is concerned, as referred to earlier in this chapter.

Obligations to employees

Initially a small company is unlikely to employ many people, but if it does so it incurs a number of legal responsibilities towards its employees. These can be grouped under two convenient heads: not to be unfairly dismissed after being employed for more than a certain number of hours each week after two year service, and to work in conditions which do not impair the employee's health and safety.

The law relating to conditions under which employees work is primarily covered in the *Offices, Shops and Railway Premises Act 1963* and the *Health and Safety at Work Act 1974*. It is not necessary with these two Acts to go into great detail; it is sufficient to note that the former does not confine itself solely to the shop or photographic studio, but to all parts of the premises used by staff, even the approaches. Floors and steps have to be cleaned at least once a week and furniture and fittings have to be kept in a clean condition.

There are also regulations which lay down the amount of space each staff member is entitled to and the minimum temperature which has to be maintained. It is also decreed that within an hour of staff commencing work, the temperature must have reached 16 degrees centigrade. Furthermore, ventilation must be adequate as must lighting and a store provided for employees to keep clothes if they have to change to carry out their duties.

The *Employers Liability (Compulsory Insurance) Act 1969* places a duty upon employers to provide insurance in respect of any injuries employees may suffer in the course of their work.

Obligations to customers

Similar obligations are imposed by law to provide for the safety of customers using a shop or photographic studio, and this is contained in the *Occupiers Liability Act 1957*. This imposes on occupiers of premises a common law duty of care to ensure visitors do not come to harm. This means premises must be reasonably safe for any visitor, whatever their status.

With a shop or photographic studio the visitor does not have to be invited in; the law assumes that where premises of this type are concerned, a person who enters them as a potential customer is assumed to have been invited in.

Even trespassers – which could include burglars – are entitled to a measure of protection under the Act. Although a trespasser enters the premises at his own risk, the occupier is expected to display a common duty of humanity, which means he is not entitled to set traps or other devices which can cause injury.

A higher standard of care is expected to be shown by occupiers towards children who may come onto the premises.

15 Loss, Insurance & Claims

It is not inappropriate to end this book with the topics of dealing with losses, obtaining insurance, and making legal claims.

Insurance in a vital element in this. All photographers, be they amateurs, part-time freelances or full time professionals, should carry appropriate insurance to reimburse themselves not only for loss, theft or damage, but also as cover against any claims which may be made against them.

Insuring equipment

Obviously all photographic equipment should be properly insured against loss, theft or damage. If equipment is included in the photographer's house contents insurance, he should be sure it is covered for anything which may happen to it when it is being used outside the house. Many household policies do not provide cover for individual items when not actually in the house, or if domestic items are found to have been used for what they deem to be "business use".

It is essential to remember that representatives of insurance companies – employees or agents – cannot be expected to read the mind of a person seeking insurance. If, as common sense dictates should be the case, expensive equipment is to be insured for various uses outside the house, it is essential for the insured person to make certain this is so.

In fact, even for the amateur, it is well worth considering taking out a special policy to cover photographic equipment on its own. As mentioned previously, there are a number of specialist companies that can provide suitable cover for both amateurs and professionals. Photographers who belong to professional or trade bodies can usually obtain this and other forms of insurance through schemes tailored for the organisation's membership.

Premises

Most household policies include cover up to a substantial amount of money for third party liability. But if the photographer is carrying out a business from his home he should declare this fact. If he is running, say, a portrait studio, he is certainly going to have more visitors to his premises than if the house was just for domestic use. This increases the risk of an accident and a subsequent claim if it was due to negligence or lack of a duty of care on the part of the photographer.

What many people who take out insurance fail to realise, with sometimes unfortunate results when a claim is repudiated, is that a policy of insurance constitutes a contract between the insurer and the insured. In fact it is rather more than that; it is what the law calls a contract *uberrimei fides*, that is one which calls for utmost faith on the part of the insured. This can be summed up as a duty to declare any facts which, if known to the insurer, would result in a risk being refused or, if accepted, at a higher premium.

For example, if a photographic studio is in an area where there have been a number of break-ins – especially if the premises has already been a victim and no claim was made on the insurance company concerned – these facts must be reported either before a new policy is taken out or an existing one renewed because such knowledge would be likely to affect the premium concerned. Nowadays, of course, with computerised assessment based on postcodes, risks in respect of burglaries, car thefts or vandalism are often arbitrarily based on the postcode. An inner city code is likely to carry a higher premium than one in a country district.

In the previous chapter the responsibilities of an employer towards staff and visitors to a shop and/or studio was dealt with. It was also noted that the law calls for employees to be covered by an employer against accidents at work and that the *Occupiers Liability*

Act 1957 imposes a duty of care on owners of land and property to ensure visitors are not injured. Those operating from business premises should ensure they have insurance cover for these aspects too.

Vehicles

The photographer who is most likely to be at risk of having an insurance claim repudiated unless all the facts have been declared is the "part-time professional".

This might be someone who works in a full time job during the week but at the weekends takes wedding photographs, for which he uses his car. The car is, in all probability, only insured for domestic and social use. This no doubt covers its use by the photographer to go to and from his regular place of work, but unless the fact has been declared, it is unlikely to cover use of the vehicle for the purpose of taking commercial wedding photographs.

Vehicles which are insured for business purposes are usually subject to a higher premium because they are considered to be on the road more often and therefore exposed to a greater risk of being involved in an accident. The part-timer who may well have to dash from one wedding to another on a Saturday afternoon, may well take risks which he would not usually take in order to get to his next assignment on time. Consequently the risk is higher and the exposure of the insurer greater.

It is therefore necessary for any photographer in this category to inform his insurer of any part-time occupation for which the car is to be used so that any additional premium can be charged.

Most complaints which are levied against insurance companies which decline to honour a claim happen as a result of the insured failing to read the small print. For instance, policies of motor insurance place an obligation on the insured to see that such vital components of a vehicle as lights, brakes and steering are kept in working order.

This proviso to the policy is usually to be found in the small print. Some years ago a motorist sued his insurance company for breach of contract when the company repudiated the policy after the motorist had been involved in an accident which happened in daylight hours. The insurers had had the damaged vehicle examined by an engineer who reported that, at the time of the accident, the lights were not in working order.

This, claimed the insurer, was a breach of a condition of the policy to keep the lights in working order, and as a result they were entitled to repudiate the policy. The insured motorist naturally argued that the defective lights had no bearing on the accident but the judge, although expressing every sympathy with the motorist, found that in law the insurers were entitled to repudiate because the motorist was in breach of the terms of his insurance.

Negatives and slides

There have been frequent instances where photographers – be they amateurs or professionals – have submitted negatives or slides to a newspaper or magazine in the hope of publication, which have been subsequently lost or damaged. Obviously it is in the interests of good relations with the contributor for the publication concerned to take care of submitted material, but with the best will in the world there is no foolproof system which offers a hundred per cent guarantee against loss or damage.

Generally it can be argued that a publication owes a common duty of care to look after submitted photographs, even those which are unsolicited. In the interest of good relations the publication may well offer a sum of money by way of recompense. However, many have a policy of refusing to do so in the case of material submitted speculatively.

As with claims against processing firms, it may be possible to quantify the cost of obtaining the photographs – travel expenses etc – but whether or not this could be claimed would depend upon the publication being told so when the photographs were submitted.

Photographers sometimes try to claim for compensation on the basis of what they think the photographs would have earned. But unless they had been commissioned and a fee agreed, it is almost impossible to quantify the fee the photographs may have fetched when published, and a publication cannot be expected to put a figure on their value sight unseen.

The moral is that if photographs are to be insured, such insurance should include loss or damage while in transit or otherwise out of the care of the photographer. Even so, insurers would be most reluctant to enter into an open ended commitment as to the commercial value of non-commissioned photographs.

Choosing insurance

Throughout this section of the book the need to have appropriate insurance has been stressed and although there are a number of specialist photographic policies it is more than likely that the average photographer – amateur or professional – will not be in a position to examine all of them. Even if he does, in many cases he may well find that none of them provide cover for all of his needs.

The most effective way to be certain that the insurance fits the requirements is for the photographer to think about what he wants insured, and in what circumstances, and then list them. This list should contain a condition that the equipment is insured whether it be in the photographer's home, studio (if he has one) or motor vehicle, and if the insurance is to include business or pleasure use or both.

An amateur photographer whose standards of photography are such that he can expect to sell some of his photographs for commercial use or for publication, would be wise to insure his equipment for use for both hobby and business purposes.

Having drawn up a list of insurance requirements, the photographer should consult a reputable broker who is a member of his trade or professional association, and let the broker know that he is relying on the broker's expertise and knowledge to get a policy which will provide cover for all the requirements which are listed.

The advantage of this method is that if something does happen and it is necessary to claim under the policy, and the insurer declined to accept responsibility and meet the claim because the particular risk was uninsured, the photographer can claim against the broker. The grounds would be that he was in breach of contract and negligent in not getting the coverage he undertook to obtain when he agreed to use his expertise and knowledge to act for the photographer.

Pursuing claims

No one should rush into litigation which, even without the expense factor, can be time-consuming and worrying. Yet there are times when litigation, or the threat of it, may be the only way in which consumer and other legal rights can be enforced.

The most consumer-friendly forum for settling legal disputes are the small claims courts which are attached to county courts. These are not actually separate courts – the term is simply used to describe the arbitration procedure used to settle disputes over relatively small amounts. Although presided over by either a deputy district judge, who is usually a lawyer who sits part time, or a full time district judge, the proceedings are informal and the use of lawyers by one side or the other is discouraged. Court staff are usually helpful and will advise on correct procedure.

Small claims courts deal with claims of up to £3,000. The court costs, which can be recovered by a winning plaintiff, vary, ranging from £10 for a claim of £100 or less up to £80 according to the amount claimed.

In Scotland the small claims limit is £750, with cases heard in the Sheriff court. In Northern Ireland the limit is £1,000.

Nevertheless, in many cases the mere threat to resort to litigation may be sufficient to encourage a settlement. Before a photographer embarks upon litigation to enforce his claim as someone who is owed money, or his rights as a consumer or for any other matter which could fall within the jurisdiction of the small claims procedure, the intention to take legal action should be notified to the other party.

In the author's view, the best way to proceed is to send by recorded delivery a letter setting out the claim and asking for payment within 14 days of receipt of the letter – failing which action will be taken in the small claims court.

This may well have the desired effect and produce either payment in full or an offer; if it does not, the potential plaintiff has to decide if to go ahead with the threat to take action. If he decides to do so, the next step is the taking out and serving of a summons. Again, this may on its own have the effect that the letter did not, and produce either payment in full or an offer.

If any offer is made the photographer must decide not only if it is one that he would feel happy with, bearing in mind that acceptance would mean that he would not have the worry of appearing in court, or if he wishes to go ahead with litigation. As user-friendly as the small claims procedure may be, it can be a worrying experience for many people. This is a decision only the claimant can make.

However if the sum of money claimed is for a debt which has either been admitted by the debtor or can be easily proved, there is no reason why anyone should take second best and accept less than is owed.

Claims between £3,000 and £5,000 will also be dealt with in the county courts, but where the amount claimed is over £5,000 the case can be heard in either a county court or in the High Court. Usually, where a large sum of money is at stake either by way of quantifiable or unquantifiable damages or a heavy debt or breach of contract, the case will be heard in the High Court. The general practice is that county courts deal with those cases where the sum claimed or at stake is not an excessively high figure.

The advantage of using a county court is that cases will come to trial far quicker than if the case is put down for trial in the High Court. Costs and legal costs are also much less.

In cases which are likely to be heard in a county court or the High Court it is essential to seek legal advice, as has been mentioned earlier. If the photographer has limited means, this can frequently be obtained from the local Citizens Advice Bureau.

Finally, it is worth remembering that many people undertake litigation which is either hopeless or of limited value only, on what they consider to be a point of principle. There is a maxim that is worth noting: "When principle comes through the door, common sense flies out the window."

Appendix I

The Press Complaints Commission

The Press Complaints Commission (PCC) is an independent organisation which succeeded the Press Council in 1991 to ensure that British newspapers and magazines follow the letter and spirit of an ethical code of practice.

It deals with some 2,500 complaints each year, many of which are dealt with by editors of the publication which is the subject of complaint, if of inaccuracy, while the remainder are adjudicated upon by the Commission. The majority of members of the PCC are independent of the press, but there are seven members who represent all sections of newspapers and magazines.

The Code of Practice, which the PCC is charged with enforcing, was framed by the newspaper and periodical publishing industries and ratified by the PCC. Its preamble states:

"All members of the press have a duty to maintain the highest professional and ethical standards. In doing so, they should have regard to the provisions of this Code of Practice and to safeguarding the public's right to know.

"Editors are responsible for the actions of journalists employed by their publications. They should also satisfy themselves as far as possible that material accepted from non-staff members was obtained in accordance with this Code.

"While recognising that this involves a substantial element of self-restraint by editors and journalists, it is designed to be acceptable in the context of a system of self-regulation. The Code applies in the spirit as well as in the letter.

"It is the responsibility of editors to co-operate as swiftly as possible in PCC enquiries. Any publication which is criticised by the PCC under one of the following clauses is duty bound to print the adjudication which follows in full and with due prominence."

The PCC Code of Practice

1. Accuracy

i) Newspapers and periodicals should take care not to publish inaccurate, misleading or distorted material.

ii) Whenever it is recognised that a significant inaccuracy, misleading statement or distorted report has been published, it should be corrected promptly and with due prominence.

iii) An apology should be published whenever appropriate.

iv) A newspaper or periodical should always report fairly and accurately the outcome of an action for defamation in which it has been a party.

2. Opportunity to reply

A fair opportunity for reply to inaccuracies should be given to individuals or when reasonably called for.

3. Comment, conjecture and fact

Newspapers, whilst free to be partisan, should distinguish clearly between comment, conjecture and fact.

4. Privacy

(i) Intrusions and enquiries into an individual's private life without his or her consent, including the use of long-lens photography to take pictures of people on private property without their consent, are only acceptable when it can be shown that these are, or reasonably believed to be, in the public interest.

(ii) Publication of material obtained under (i) above is only justified when the facts show that the public interest is served.

Note: Private property is defined as (i) any private residence, together with its gardens and outbuildings, but excluding any adjacent fields or parkland and the surrounding part of the property within the unaided view of passers-by, (ii) hotel bedrooms (but not other areas in a hotel and (iii) those parts of a hospital or nursing home where patients are treated or accommodated.

5. Listening devices

Unless justified by the public interest, journalists should not obtain or publish material obtained by using clandestine listening devices or by intercepting private telephone conversations.

6. Hospitals

i) Journalists or photographers making enquiries at hospitals or similar institutionss should identify themselves to a responsible executive and obtain permission before entering non-public areas.
ii) The restrictions on intruding into privacy are particularly relevant to enquiries about individuals in hospitals or similar institutions.

7. Misrepresentation

i) Journalists should not generally obtain or seek to obtain information or pictures through misrepresentation or subterfuge.
ii) Unless in the public interest, documents or photographs should be removed only with the express consent of the owner.
iii) Subterfuge can be justified only in the public interest and only when material cannot be obtained by any other means.

8. Harassment

i) Journalists should neither obtain nor seek to obtain information or pictures through intimidation or harassment.
ii) Unless their enquiries are in the public interest, journalists should not photograph individuals on private property (as defined in the note to Clause 4) without consent; should not persist in telephoning or questioning individuals after having been asked to desist; should not remain on their property after having been asked to leave and should not follow them.

iii) It is the responsibility of editors to ensure these requirements are carried out.

9. Payment for articles

(i) Payment or offers of payment for stories or information should not be made directly or through agents to witnesses or potential witnesses in current criminal proceedings except where the material concerned ought to be published in the public interest and there is an overriding need to make or promise to make a payment for this to be done. Journalists must take every possible step to ensure that no financial dealings have influence on the evidence that those witnesses may give.

(An editor authorising such a payment must be prepared to demonstrate that there is a legitimate public interest at stake involving matters that the public has a right to know. The payment, or where accepted, the offer of payment to any witness who is actually cited to give evidence should be disclosed to the prosecution and the defence and the witness advised of this.)

(ii) Payment or offers of payment for stories, pictures or information, should not be made directly or through agents to convicted or confessed criminals or to their associates – who may include family, friends and colleagues – except where the material concerned ought to be published in the public interest and payment is necessary for this to be done

10. Intrusion into grief or shock

In cases involving personal grief or shock, enquiries should be carried out and approaches made with sympathy and discretion.

11. Innocent relatives and friends

Unless it is contrary to the public's right to know, the press should avoid identifying relatives or friends of persons convicted or accused of crime.

12. Interviewing or photographing children

i) Journalists should not normally interview of photograph children under the age of 16 on subjects involving the personal welfare of the child or any other child in the absence of or without the consent of a parent or other adult who is responsible for the children.

ii) Children should not be approached or photographed while at school without the permission of the school authorities.

13. Children in sex cases

1. The press should not, even where the law does not prohibit it, identify children under the age of 16 who are involved in cases concerning sexual offences, whether as victims or as witnesses or defendants.

2. In any press report of a case involving a sexual offence against a child –

i) The adult should be identified.

ii) The word "incest" should be avoided where a child victim might be identified.

iii) The offence should be described as "serious offences against young children" or similar appropriate wording.

iv) The child should not be identified.

v) Care should be taken that nothing in the report implies the relationship between the accused and the child.

14. Victims of crime

The press should not identify victims of sexual assault or publish material likely to contribute to such identification unless, by law, they are free to do so.

15. Discrimination

i) The press should avoid prejudicial or pejorative reference to a person's race, colour, religion, sex or sexual orientation or to any physical or mental illness or disability.

ii) It should avoid publishing details of a person's race, colour, or sexual orientation unless they are directly relevant to the story.

16. Financial journalism

i) Even where the law does not prohibit it, journalists should not use for their own profit financial information they receive in advance of its general publication, nor should they pass such information to others.

ii) They should not write about those shares or securities in whose performance they know that they or their close families have a significant financial interest without disclosing the interest to the editor or financial editor.

iii) They should not buy or sell, either directly or through nominees or agents, shares or securities about which they have written recently or about which they intend to write in the near future.

17. Confidential sources

Journalists have a moral obligation to protect confidential sources of information.

18. The public interest

Clauses 4, 5, 7, 8 and 9 create exceptions which may be covered by invoking the public interest. For the purpose of this Code that is most easily defined as:

i) Detecting or exposing crime or a serious misdemeanour.

ii) Protecting public health and safety.

iii) Preventing the public from being misled by some statement or action of an individual or organisation.

In cases raising issues beyond these three definitions the Press Complaints Commission will require a full explanation by the editor of the publication involved, seeking to demonstrate how the public interest was served.

Wildlife photography and protected species

Further to the situation outlined in Chapter 11, this section summarises the guidelines for photographing wildlife provided by English Nature, and lists protected species.

For birds, English Nature sets out the legal and practical requirements which are needed for photography, together with the standard of ability English Nature expects would-be bird photographers to obtain before being granted a licence to take photographs of specially protected birds.

Photographing common species of birds

Generally all species can be photographed away from the nest, but while many bird photographers will be content to restrict their photography of wild birds to either chance or opportune moments, some will wish to photograph a wide range of bird species or even seek to do the impossible – get a perfect shot.

Noting that the majority of would-be wildlife photographers will possess such basic equipment as a lightweight automatic camera and will be content to take photographs when the opportunity presents itself, English Nature says it is unlikely this type of photographer will set out to take a close-up of a bird unless it is particularly attractive or easily accessible to the photographer.

The basic rules include the acknowledgment that the interests and welfare of the birds are paramount, that there is an avoidance of any undue disturbance to the bird or damage to its habitat, and that the instructions of landowners/occupiers as well as the Country Code are observed.

For most photographers it is considered that this will be a matter of common sense, but it is recognised that exuberance or over-enthusiasm can bring all photographers into disrepute. Specialised bird photography is likely to be followed by those who have a degree of interest in birds and wish to take photographs for aesthetic and identification purposes, or with a view to publication. This, observes English Nature, will almost certainly involve attempts to get nearer to individual birds.

Normally, and providing the normal rules of good practice are followed, there will be no detriment to wildlife purely for the benefit of the photographer. It is anticipated that those wishing to photograph scarce or rare breeding birds will build up a portfolio of species at or near the nest, enabling knowledge of species and reactions of individual birds to be accrued. This should be accompanied by expertise on how to approach certain species and gain the best photographic results with minimal effect on the birds.   In taking good quality photographs of birds at the nest, it is expected that extreme care will be taken not to cause any undue disturbance. This includes not only being as quiet as possible, but ensuring that the creation of hides, or the route taken to the nest at each visit, does not become so familiar as to pinpoint the location of the nest site for both human and natural predators.

Any work carried out at a colony, or on a colonial nesting species (e.g. terns, gulls, sand martins, etc) should always be in conjunction or co-operation with those who are organising nest protection or monitoring schemes.

For some birds a slight amount of "gardening" - the interference with or reduction in the cover of the nest – may be necessary. In all cases this should be the minimum necessary for the purpose of the proposed photograph whilst still maintaining the integrity and protection of the nest site.

The nest should be exposed for no longer than is absolutely necessary at any time, to other people, predators or adverse weather conditions. Any removal of the nest cover should be temporary and achieved by tying back rather than cutting off or displacing vegetation, which should be fully restored as soon as possible once sufficient photographs have been taken.

Protection of Schedule 1 species

The provisions of Schedule 1 apply to species on that Schedule in the breeding season when the birds are at or near nests, or when there are dependent young in the nest. Thus a Peregrine, for example, which is a Schedule 1 species, may be photographed at any time of the year away from the nest or nest site. The legislation relating to Schedule 1 species is applicable to people wishing to intentionally disturb a scheduled species at or near the nest for the purpose of photography.

Species on Schedule 1 can only be disturbed, for photography or any other purposes, when a licence has been issued by English Nature. The applicant will need to demonstrate some photographic experience gained from having photographed several common species and the provision of photographs of at least six different species at the nest. The names of two referees who can comment on his ability, both in conservation and photographic terms, should also be provided.

For some species English Nature operates a quota system restricting the number of licences issued. This is in cases where the species requested by the applicant are very scarce, such as the Firecrest, or, like the Dartford Warbler, have a restricted breeding range. Quotas are usually based on the conservation status of the species, their sensitivity to disturbance and the likely demand for licences. For some species the quota will be nil, whilst others will be restricted within particular, named areas.

Provided that applicants give sufficiently early notice of their application at the start of the year, most photographers' wishes will be accommodated. If not they will be informed of a refusal in good time to make other plans. While it is regretted that some disappointments may result in some cases, the reasons behind English Nature's allocation of licences must be borne in mind, with the conservation status of the species paramount.

Licences will not be given at short notice but the English Nature licensing section will try to provide every effort to late applicants in order to let them know of decisions so they can make alternative arrangements. It may also be possible for holders of photography licences to add a species to the licence at a late stage – perhaps having discovered a nest unexpectedly – providing there is room on the quota.

It must be emphasised that photography of Schedule 1 species involves considerable preparation in locating the nest, determining the best method of photographing the nest, the erection and positioning of any hides, as well as the avoidance of giving away the nest location to predators.

Erection of a hide, particularly for extremely sensitive species such as birds of prey, will probably have to be carried out some way from the nest and introduced by slowly moving it into the final desired position allowing the birds to become acclimatised to its presence. Only in exceptional circumstances should a hide be left in place for longer than is required by the individual photographer, and removal should be at the earliest opportunity once the operation is completed.

English Nature anticipates that most licences issued to photographers of Schedule 1 birds at the nest will be used in conjunction with hide photography. The photography of a few species will not be practical in this way, but always photographers are asked to ensure that the most appropriate way of taking photographs is carried out with the minimal disturbance to the bird in question.

Any action which may leads to the abandonment of the nest site by the bird should be prevented and any activity either by a licence holder or by third parties which may lead to the detriment of the bird or its nest should be the subject of a report to English Nature's licensing section as soon as possible.

English Nature also asks that at the end of the licensing period – usually the 30th September – licence holders submit reports on their activities at or near the nest giving the number of visits and, if this fact is known, whether the nest was successful or not.

Further guidance

Another useful leaflet called *The Nature Photographers' Code of Practice* has also been prepared by English Nature in co-operation with the Nature Group of the Royal Photographic Society. This mentions remote-control photographic work of birds at the nest. Where this involves resetting a shutter or moving a film on manually between exposures, it is even less likely to be acceptable because of the frequency of disturbance involved.

The leaflet also includes the photographing of mammals away from the nest or burrow and the care that is needed if it is necessary to disturb animals during the hibernation period.

Where protected plants are concerned, the leaflet comments that photographers should be clear about existing protective legislation. Without the permission of the landowner (or his tenant) it can be an offence to uproot any wild plant where "gardening" is involved in pursuit of nature photography.

There are less than a hundred plants which are considered to be very threatened, and these include the rarest orchids which grow in this country. In respect of these plants the law extends to picking, so any damage to surrounding vegetation which a photographer may cause must be avoided.

The leaflet observes: "If photography comes to be seen as a threat rather than an aid to rare plant conservation, pressures may mount for more restrictive legislation such as giving protected plants at flowering time similar protection to that enjoyed by Schedule 1 birds at nesting time.

"No rarity should be plucked, still less dug up, for studio photography or to facilitate the *in situ* photography of another specimen. Nor should one part be removed to facilitate the photography of another part."

Copies of these and other leaflets are available from the RPS at The Octagon, Milsom Street, Bath BA1 1DN, or from English Nature, Northminster House, Peterborough PE1 1AU.

Index